TEN KEYS TO

LATIN AMERICA

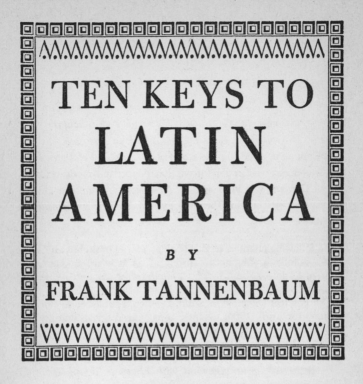

TEN KEYS TO LATIN AMERICA

BY

FRANK TANNENBAUM

VINTAGE BOOKS

A Division of Random House

NEW YORK

Prefatory Note

A BOOK such as this can be written only after many years' association with the people it describes. I would not know how to acknowledge my indebtedness because I have been favored by so many over so long a time.

It is difficult, perhaps impossible, for anyone, especially an outsider, to understand and evaluate the major facets of a culture. This is a book about the totality of Latin America. The Ten Keys are merely ten different angles of vision. The whole is more complex than the sum of the parts.

FRANK TANNENBAUM

Columbia University
New York, New York
May 14, 1962

CONTENTS

TEN KEYS TO

LATIN AMERICA

CHAPTER 1

THE LAND AND THE PEOPLE

1. Contrasts and Identities

DON FEDERICO DE ONÍS, for so many years the leading influence in Hispanic studies in the United States, likes to say that he can always recognize an American in Paris but cannot tell whether he comes from New York or Buenos Aires, from Chicago or Caracas. There is something about his bearing—the way he holds his head, his swinging arms and long strides, the innocence and optimism reflected in every gesture—which marks him as a child of the New World. This is one way of saying that Americans North and South are in some measure interchangeable, that their history has molded them in a similar if not identical crucible. The familiar list of differences between the United States and Latin America is only partially true. Four centuries of a common heritage have given all of us "something" marked as American rather than European. It is discernible in our prose and poetry, in our politics, in our attitude toward the outside world, in our popular heroes and folk tales, in the stories we tell our children, and in the moral issues that trouble the grown-up.

That "something" comes from the universal American experience with the Indian, the Negro, the open spaces and wide horizons, the unique role of the horse (the cowboy, the *gaucho*, the *llanero*, the *charro* are all brothers under the skin), and the experiences of ranch life—driving cattle a thousand miles, as is still done in Brazil, for instance. The tradition of a culture uprooted in the Old World and replanted in the New is shared by all our people. The mixture of races from many parts of the globe, the continuing flow of immigrants and their rapid conversion into something different from what they were, a high degree of social and physical mobility—all are part of a common tradition. Our pride and self-confidence arise out of a world that can still be easily molded—a world that has been derived from the historic American belief in progress and from the notion that government belongs to the people and is a human and malleable instrument which yields to pressure and is subject to change at the ballot box or by a "revolution." All of the nations in this hemisphere achieved their independence by rebellion, and our early national heroes were all "rebels" against a king in the Old World. Our American belief in self-government is evident even in areas where the *caudillo* or the political "boss" is a continuing and sometimes a sinister figure, and most of our popular upheavals have been in the name of democracy.

These traditions, shared in different degrees and varying

forms, have given the people on this side of the Atlantic a view of the world, a sense of the ways of man with nature and his fellows, and a psychological and spiritual heritage in common. This identity is deeper than the obvious differences which separate us. An extension of this is our feeling of isolation from the rest of the world and our awareness of separation from Europe and Asia. It is no accident that the inter-American system, a half-century old, is now the world's oldest international political organization.

Our common history has given us our cultural similarities and, to a large degree, what the anthropologist would call a "similar character structure." But the contrasts are also marked and frequently commented upon. Despite our common origin in Europe, the conquerors and settlers of Central and South America have had a different and more difficult history than the North Americans. They have had a harder route to travel from the day they established their first colony to their present position as sovereign nations.

For one thing, the West Indies and Central and South America have proved less propitious to human habitation than the United States. Latin America is more isolated from the rest of the world, more tropical, more mountainous, and has proportionately less good farming land. South America—more than twice the size of the United States, including Alaska—faces Africa rather than Europe and lies at a greater distance from China, India, the Middle East, and Europe. Until the opening of the Panama Canal, a ship from North America or Europe had to go around Cape Horn to reach the ports of Valparaiso in Chile or Callao in Peru. And until the airplane became an easy means of travel, businessmen and diplomats going from Lima, Quito, or Bogotá to Europe would travel via

New York. Through the centuries, South America and Central America lay outside the normal trade routes, and it is still almost impossible to go from Panama to the east coast of South America by boat.

South America stretches 4,500 miles from north to south and about 3,000 miles from east to west. The west coast is blocked off from the rest of the continent by a mountain range that, paralleling the ocean, runs without a break from Venezuela to the southern tip of Chile, or the entire 4,500 miles. The Andes reach 23,000 feet at the peak of Aconcagua in Chile and over 21,000 feet at Illampu and Illimani in Bolivia, while Ecuador's Chimborazo, at 20,700 feet, was for a long time believed even higher than Aconcagua. There are dozens of mountain peaks over 16,000 feet high, and the snowline in Bolivia lies between 16,000 and 18,000 feet. In Peru and Bolivia an entire chain of white mountain peaks stretches as far as the eye can see. These snow-capped mountains lie in the tropics, in the latitude of the Belgian Congo, Tanganyika, Mozambique, and Indonesia. As a result, the Andes, as well as mountains in Central America and Mexico, have the odd feature of combining perpetual snow with endless heat. One can, when the road is good, go from Guayaquil in Ecuador to the foothills of Chimborazo or from Acapulco halfway up the lower range of Popocatepetl in Mexico in a few hours. Central American and a large part of South American culture is influenced by this proximity of the tropical world to temperate climates, and by the ease with which one can go down to the heat and moisture of the tropics, or up to the cool, dry, and often cold and barren mountain valley, or have a house that is only a few hours away from both climates. The fact that one goes up or down to meet sharp

changes in climate and consequent changes in food, clothing, and shelter is a significant factor in Latin American
culture. These unique contrasts multiply and enrich human experiences, but they also add to its difficulties. The
Andean mountain chain is like a wall three to four miles
high, stretching the entire length of the continent from
north to south. The passes are few and, except in the extreme south, higher than 12,000 feet; most are 14,000 feet
or more. A pass in the Andes is usually a narrow winding
strip along the bank of some mountain stream rushing
down from the heights. The mule trail, railroad, and more
recent automobile road must all crowd the same steep,
circuitous slit eroded through the centuries, competing for
space against the towering ledge. It is worth emphasizing
this point—and anyone who has gone by automobile from
Lima to Cerro de Pasco or Tingo María will appreciate its
significance. These are not trade routes for extensive and
heavy traffic; they are skilled and ingenious engineering
performances. They are not, except in a limited sense,
means of communication between the west coast of South
America and the other side of the mountains; they are
certainly not commercial routes between the Pacific and
the Atlantic—and are not likely to become so.

The Andes, with a mean altitude of from 14,000 to 16,000
feet for 80,000 square miles, vary in breadth from some
500 miles in Bolivia to perhaps 120 in Ecuador. The range
runs for thousands of miles in two major spurs, and in
Colombia in three—eastern, central, and western—so that
even if there were not innumerable minor mountain folds,
to go from the Colombian port of Buenaventura on the
Pacific to Bogotá, the capital, one would still have to make
three separate climbs. The west coast north of the equator

has heavy rains, but below the equator the Pacific slope, from northern Peru to central Chile, is desert, so dry, sandy, and windblown that neither bird nor insect will survive in it. Only in the few rather narrow river valleys, which fan out on reaching the coast, is life possible. Lima lies in one of these valleys, and all of coastal Peru's urban and agricultural existence depends on water flowing down through some gorge in a widening stream before it reaches the coast.

In the Andes themselves, human life tends to be pocketed in valleys 6,000 to 14,000 feet above sea level and overhung by surrounding peaks. This is true of Quito, Bogotá, La Paz, Cuzco, and even Caracas, which lies a stone's throw from the coast. The smaller towns and villages in the Andes are each isolated little pockets where men have congregated to find shelter and warmth and enough moisture to nourish animal and plant life. On the whole, however, the Andes have insufficient rain, and in many places agriculture depends upon irrigation.

Once over the divide, the traveler on the east side of the Andes looks down into the Amazonian basin many thousands of feet below, and soon runs into unceasing rain. For one crossing the divide on foot or muleback, it is a dramatic experience to pass so suddenly from a relatively dry and barren world to one where the atmosphere is moisture-ridden and the soil soggy. As the traveler comes down to about 10,000 feet, he finds himself in a boundless forest soaked by a seemingly never-ending rain. And if the rain stops, as it does now and then for a little while, the heat is so great that the soaked earth gives off a warm steamlike vapor.

The rains become less oppressive and more irregular as

one descends to 3,000 feet, and by the time one reaches the river, the rains, though still frequent, are of lesser intensity. This rain forest, *la montaña* as it is called, stretches along the Amazonian headwaters from Colombia to Bolivia. The slope of the mountain is practically uninhabited. As one gets closer to the river where the land flattens out and the rains abate, sparsely settled Indian communities are to be found. Farther south, along the eastern Andes in Santa Cruz de la Sierra and into the Pilcomayo River basin, the rain diminishes sharply and human settlements are more common.

East of the *montaña* and below it is the Amazon Basin. The Amazon Basin is estimated at 2,000,000 square miles, about as large as the United States. The Amazon itself is longer than the distance between New York and Liverpool. One of its great tributaries, the Mamoré-Madeira, is about 3,000 miles long and six others are each over 1,000 miles in length. Here is a vast river system, with an estimated 40,000 miles of navigable waters. The entire Amazon Basin lies barely above sea level. The little hamlet of Napo in Ecuador, some 2,600 miles from the Atlantic, stands only 1,600 feet above sea level, and Manaus, 1,000 miles from the mouth of the Amazon, is only 100 feet above sea level. The river falls only about one-eighth of an inch per mile for the last 500 miles of its course to the sea. The region's high temperatures inhibit the formation of fungi and the growth of humus needed for fertility, and its rains are so heavy that they leach the soil of soluble minerals. It is not a productive area agriculturally, and is poorly adapted for human habitation.

It should be added that South America has three other river systems which, if not as great as the Amazon, are formidable by any standards: the Río de la Plata, empty-ing into the Atlantic at Buenos Aires, the Orinoco, dividing Venezuela in half, and the Río Magdalena, for centuries the main route from the Colombian coast to Bogotá.

Interesting for future development is the fact that these river basins constitute a single drainage system. The in-dividual streams that make up the Río de la Plata and those that ultimately pour out into the Amazon are often so close at their point of origin that the idea of connecting these interior waterways by a short canal has been voiced many times. Similarly, the Orinoco and the Amazon have been examined as a possible interior water route. Except for other factors, it would be perfectly feasible to take a canoe up the Orinoco, through the Casiquiare into the Río Negro to the Amazon at Manaus, and from there pick any one of a number of rivers that, with a portage of a few miles, would enable one to float down into the Río de la Plata and out to the Atlantic near Buenos Aires.

As we reach the east coast we find a steep mountain range that rises to 10,000 feet and has an average height of about 4,000 feet. This escarpment is close to the sea and runs for some 1,700 miles from north to south, almost the entire length of Brazil. Between the Andes on the west, the Brazilian highlands on the east, the Amazonian rivers and forest on the north, the interior of South America is diffi-cult to penetrate, to cross, or to abide in. The Amazonian forests that stretch endlessly along the rivers and cover the western mountains are more difficult to traverse than the Sahara Desert. Only the rivers give access to the interior, and so far they have not induced extensive internal settle-ment.

In southern Brazil we enter a temperate zone, and as we reach Argentina we are in a treeless Pampa, flat, rich in good soils, with adequate rains and an almost ideal climate. These good lands, however, are comparatively limited, become drier as one goes west, and long before reaching the foothills of the Andes, one sees irrigation ditches. The continent narrows sharply below the province of Buenos Aires, and Patagonia has to date, like the Amazon Basin, remained for most of mankind an unknown mysterious world.

Most of South America lies within the Equatorial Zone —from a latitude 30° North of the Equator to 30° South— and most of North America lies outside it. South America is like Africa; North America, like Europe. Only about 8 per cent of Europe has a mean annual temperature of between 60° and 70° Fahrenheit while 66 per cent of South America has over 70° and 20 per cent over 80° Fahrenheit. The high temperature is compounded by the heavy rains. Both the Amazon Basin and central Brazil have between 70 and 80 inches of rain a year. The La Plata area has adequate rain and temperatures that fall below 70°. Southern Chile is rainy and cool, while the coast between Panama and Ecuador is rainy and hot—it has one of the heaviest annual rainfalls on earth. Mexico and Central America, like South America, are relatively cool in the mountains, with ideal temperatures, but almost always hot and wet on the coast. A similar generalization may be made about the West Indies—cool in the mountains and wet and humid on the coast.

2. The Land and the People

This rather long description of the land is essential if one is to understand the political, economic, and social conditions of Latin America. What it teaches us is that the area is isolated from the world and isolated internally. It has always been easier to go to the United States from Lima or Rio de Janeiro than to go overland from the capital of Peru to the capital of Brazil. The interior of South America is empty. It has been asserted that in the Amazon Basin, whose vast extent covers half the territory of Brazil, Venezuela, Colombia, Equador, Peru, Bolivia, and Paraguay, there are fewer than two people per square mile. In British, French, and Dutch Guiana, Patagonia, and the Atacama Desert, human settlement is equally sparse.

The vast majority of the 135,000,000 people in South America live within 200 miles of the coast. All of the really big cities lie at the edge of the Pacific or Atlantic Ocean— Montevideo, Buenos Aires, São Paulo, Rio de Janeiro, Caracas, Lima, Callao, Guayaquil, Valparaiso, and Santiago. Bogotá, Quito, and La Paz, though 100 to 200 miles inland, are oriented toward the coast. The great urban centers face out toward the sea and not toward the interior. There is no St. Louis, Chicago, Minneapolis, Denver, and Salt Lake City in the center of South America. In all of the Amazon Basin there is only Belém with 230,000, Manaus, a thousand miles up the river, with 100,000 people, and another thousand miles farther up and serving as the commercial center for the upper Amazon, Iquitos with about 42,000.

Latin America as a whole has something close to 193,-000,000 people as of 1959, scattered over more than 7,769,-247 square miles—about 25 persons per square mile as against 57 in the United States. The population in the Western Hemisphere has been growing at a more rapid rate than in any other part of the world, and Latin America's rate is almost twice that of the United States and Canada combined. Between 1920 and 1955 the population south of the United States more than doubled—from 90,-000,000 to 183,000,000. Taking the record of population growth in recent times, demographers estimate "conservatively" that by the end of this century there will be nearly 600,000,000 human beings south of the United States border and only about half of that number north of it.

If the Mexican experience is used as a pattern for Latin America, then the rate of growth in the near future promises to be higher than it has been in the recent past. In 1956 the Mexican birth rate was nearly twice as high as that in the United States, while the death rate had fallen by 43 per cent since 1940. The net gain in population is now about 1,000,000 a year. In 1956 Mexico had 30,500,-000 people, and with the declining death rate, its population will be increasing by 3.5 per cent a year, thereby doubling itself, for at least the next two generations, every twenty years. This will mean something like 100,000,000 Mexicans at the end of the century. On the basis of the record, there is little that man can do about this, and it seems certain that he will fail to do the little he could. We must, therefore, assume that what is happening in Mexico will in all probability happen in Central America, on the islands of the Caribbean, and in South America. The population which, before the First World War, was kept in check by a high death rate has now entered a period of rapid expansion.

The reason for this sudden increase of the population is to be found in the improved health practices of the last fifty years. About half the area traditionally affected by malaria has been cleared. For the first time man is free of that dread disease in many parts of Latin America. A campaign waged against yellow fever in the larger cities of Brazil, Ecuador, Peru, Panama, Bolivia, Nicaragua, and Paraguay was strikingly successful and was helped along by the simultaneous campaign against malaria, since both programs used DDT spraying to combat disease-carrying mosquitoes. The incidence of smallpox, so deadly to the American Indian, has in recent years been reduced by about half. Some twenty-five years ago on a muleback trip over the mountains in one Latin American country, I remember walking into a rural school and finding it nearly empty. "Where are your children?" I asked, and the teacher, a sad young woman, replied: "They all died of smallpox." "What did you do?" "Ay Señor, I sent a message to the authorities in the county seat (about two days away by horseback) but I never got an answer." This incident is a measure of the change that has occurred, for it would be difficult, if not impossible, to repeat this experience today. The public health authorities are better trained, better financed, and, most important of all, public health campaigns have increased the awareness of the people and the sense of responsibility and professional pride of the authorities. A campaign in Haiti against yaws has brought that crippling disease under control, and similar efforts are under way in other countries.

Increased life expectancy, decreased mortality especially among children, better health, and evidence of improved public sanitation have all come in the wake of recent changes in medical practice. What is important to keep in mind is that these developments are taking place even in countries where there have been few signs of comparable economic development.

The use of DDT has worked marvels in mosquito control. In Ciudad Bolívar on the Orinoco in Venezuela where malarial incidence was almost universal, it has been entirely eliminated. I saw people playing tennis there at night under large headlights and I slept without a mosquito net—something unheard of a few years ago. All of this was the result of a systematic spraying of all the houses every few months. A doctor with a few assistants goes up and down the river in a small launch, bringing the benefit of DDT to all the houses along the shores and to all the river towns. The campaign is easy and inexpensive. Another important change is the availability of antibiotics. These, however, are more costly, require greater medical facilities, and call for more co-operation from the individual members of the community. But these too have been of great use in specific areas—as in the case of yaws in Haiti.

The effect of this improved health care is an increase in the number of aged and children. For a considerable time to come, the old will require a disproportionate share of nurses, doctors, medicines, and hospitals, while the young will keep their mothers busy and, among many other services, will require school buildings, school materials, books, and teachers. The increasing numbers of old and young will make it more difficult to turn from a subsistence to an industrial economy because it will be harder to save for capital investment. At the same time the need for greater productivity will increase while the means will be reduced. In proportion to the total population, the labor force will decline and the need for subsistence spending will expand.

Urbanization, true enough, affects the birth rate. Mothers aged 45 or older average 5.4 children in the city of San Juan and 7.5 in rural sections of Puerto Rico. Similarly in Brazil the figures are 6.1 to 8.0 for urban as against rural. And this difference holds true substantially everywhere— 5 to 8 in Venezuela, 4 to 8 in Costa Rica, etc. Roughly, the number of children under five is about twice as high in the country districts as it is in the cities. The rapid urbanization of Latin America may eventually decrease the birth rate. But in the near future no sudden or rapid decline in the birth rate is likely to occur. For one thing, a rural economy is still dominant, and the population is growing so fast that, for a long time to come, industrialization will barely affect the numbers of people living in rural districts.

It is, therefore, of unusual interest to note that only 5 per cent of the area of South America is in tillage or tree crops as against 20 per cent in the United States. Comparable figures for Mexico are 10 per cent, for Central America 9 per cent, and for the Antilean republics 16 per cent. Nearly 50 per cent of Latin American lands are in forest. Nearly 30 per cent are unused or unusable, and the rest are in pasture and meadows. In some ways South America represents what the United States would have been if its people had never crossed the Appalachians. This can best be illustrated by some figures. In Brazil 89 per cent of the population and an even higher percentage of the railroads and the land under cultivation are in the coastal area. After 400 years Brazil is still living on the coast, and only a fraction of its total energies have been directed over the steep escarpments toward the interior. In Argentina one third of the population is in greater Buenos Aires and is increasing at a faster rate than the rest of the country. Montevideo has more than half of

Uruguay's population. It is almost a universal rule in Latin America that the vast majority of the population occupies a fraction of each country's territory. In Bolivia, 80 per cent of the population lives on 15 per cent of the land, in Colombia half of the population is concentrated on an eighth of the land surface, and in Brazil half the people occupy one twentieth of the country. Very much the same can be said about Mexico, the Central American republics (except El Salvador), and Venezuela. On the east coast of South America the people live close by the sea. In Mexico, Central America, and the west coast of South America, they occupy the mountains. Of the more than 150 towns in Bolivia, 73 are over 12,000 feet above sea level, 26 over 13,000 feet, four over 14,000 feet, and one is over 15,700 feet. In Peru the capitals of the provinces average 9,000 feet in altitude. Comparable figures could be given for all of the countries bordering on the Pacific, except Chile. In Mexico most of the towns are located on the central plateau between 6,000 and 9,000 feet above sea level.

Despite its vast spaces and underpopulated regions, Latin America has not attracted the number of Europeans it could have absorbed. During the colonial period Spanish policy did not favor immigration even from Spain. Since independence, political instability, large landholding systems, peonage, sharply drawn social distinctions, an emphasis on luxury and ostentation rather than on investment in productive enterprises, a certain contempt for people who work with their hands, a certain religious exclusiveness which resisted open toleration of non-Catholic denominations, and finally a low standard of living all combined to divert the great European migratory move-

ment to the United States, Canada, Australia, and New
Zealand. The exceptions are Argentina, southern Brazil,
and southern Chile. But in Chile European immigration
was short-lived, and consisted mainly of Germans who
settled in the uninhabited lake and forest areas around
Puerto Montt and Puerto Varas.

In southern Brazil and Argentina, immigrants were
primarily Italian, Spanish, and Portuguese. Probably less
than 10,000,000 remained, in contrast to the 50,000,000
who settled in the United States between 1820 and 1950.
The immigrant stayed away from most of Latin America
for the same reason that Europeans coming to the United
States avoided the South. They could not compete with
the Negro and the poor white. In most places in Latin
America the Indian was as effective in keeping the European immigrant from seeking a place to settle as the
Negro had been in our own South.

I was once told by the Chinese Minister in Guatemala
that the Chinese coolie would turn peddler and petty
merchant rather than accept the conditions of life and
labor that were the Indian's portion. And these general
considerations still apply. Every effort to open South
America to refugee migration has broken down. Such
traditionally open countries as Argentina and Brazil have
accepted a small number of European refugees; the rest,
with the exception of Venezuela, almost none.

In Central America and Mexico, only Mexico has welcomed immigrants, and these were chiefly Spaniards
driven from their homes by the civil war. During the
nineteenth century there was a large-scale Spanish migration to Cuba. But on the whole, Latin America has not
welcomed European migrations and is likely to be even

less open to foreigners within the foreseeable future. The rapid population growth and a sensitive nationalism are sufficient to justify this forecast. Only if there were a very sudden and very large industrial expansion might there be a change in this isolationist attitude.

Of Latin America's 12,000,000 immigrants, not all of whom have remained, 4,000,000 were Spanish, 4,000,000 Italian, 2,000,000 Portuguese, the rest Germans, Poles, and English. Since about 1900, 300,000 Japanese have come to South America, mainly to Brazil. About half a million immigrants from India have settled in the British and Dutch Guianas and the West Indies. Paraguay has welcomed small numbers of Mennonites, Hutterites, and a small Swiss colony. Some thousands of Chinese migrants have entered Peru, Mexico, Cuba, and Trinidad.

The limited migration to Latin America reflects not only a certain social exclusiveness but an attitude that has made assimilation difficult. A foreign doctor in a city like La Paz, Quito, or Arequipa remains a foreign doctor all his life, and his children and grandchildren, even if inter-married, would be described as the children or grand children of a German, Frenchman, or American. This is not exclusiveness merely. There has been no room at the top. The idea of an expanding, flexible society and economy has not occurred to anyone.

When Sergio Bagú says that modern Argentina was born with the coming of the immigrant, his observation also applies to other countries. It is certainly true of São Paulo and to a measurable degree of other places. Before the First World War—and perhaps up to the Second World War—very nearly all the active business and industrial establishments were developed and administered by Europeans, North Americans, or by people from Lebanon and the Near East. If the English and the Americans owned and managed most of the public utilities, mines, and larger factories, the commercial places like department stores would most likely be French, the cutlery and hardware German, hotels Spanish, retail stores often Lebanese. The point is that the *criollo* lacked both the inclination and the outlook necessary for an active business career. In most instances the mestizo and mulatto had not yet moved far enough up the economic ladder to have the capital or the training necessary for operating even a small business. The Indians and Negroes had little interest in commerce and at best engaged in petty parochial transactions. As a result, the economic development of Latin America fell to foreigners by default. There was no one else to undertake it. This makes it all the more surprising that, with the exceptions noted above, immigrants should have received such meager welcome. But this is too complex a matter for a simple explanation. Immigrants were frowned upon not because they were businessmen, large or small, but because they were foreigners. And being a foreigner in a static, stratified, and authoritarian society is like being a sore finger in a good hand—always in the way, always annoying.

Like immigration, formal efforts at colonization have not prospered in the Andean countries, Central America, and Mexico. In the Andes those who have ventured over the mountains to seek a home along the eastern slope overlooking the Amazonian basin have met with scant success. Attempts in both Peru and Bolivia have, to say the least, been disappointing. This can also be said of Brazilian efforts along the Amazon and in the far interior.

The reasons are numerous, and the debate over the future prospects of the interior of South America as a center of colonization is an old one, going back at least to the early nineteenth century. To date the pessimists have been sustained in their view. But the desire for growth and expansion persists, and today rests its case on modern medicine, on DDT, on possibilities of refrigeration, on the airplane, on improved road, rail, and river communication, and most of all, perhaps, on the growth of the population. But to anyone who has traveled in the *montaña* and the upper reaches of the Amazon and has experienced the continuous rains, the floods, the heat and the humidity, and the sheer isolation and distance, the prospect must remain slim, the cost high, and the time distant. In the next few generations, only a miracle could populate the now empty spaces of the eastern Andes and that half of South America that roughly falls within the Amazonian belt, and make them flourish. And this judgment is but slightly affected by such developments as the iron mines on the Curane River in the Orinoco delta in Venezuela, the Tingo María agricultural settlement in eastern Peru, or the oil explorations in the Bolivian Chaco. These are all important to the total economy of the nations involved, but they are tiny specks in a vast land.

3. Provincial Isolation

The impact of mountain, desert, and jungle on the history, politics, and social organization of the area has been profound. Almost nowhere in Latin America does one find men living in the countryside and in the spaces between the towns. Latin America consists of cities, towns, and villages, with almost no human habitation in between. This is true almost everywhere—in the tropics, the mountains, the coast, or the plain. Buenos Aires, Quito, Lima, and Caracas are all large cities surrounded by human vacuums. This is also true of Cuzco and Arequipa, of Cuenca and Ibarra, of Zacatecas and Chihuahua, and of the thousands of smaller towns and villages.

The large city is impressive and dominating, but in Mexico, for example, there are over 100,000 little villages, the vast majority with no more than 400 inhabitants. Ninety-nine per cent of all Mexican towns have fewer than 2,000 people. So it is almost everywhere.

The thousands of provincial capitals, pueblos, villages, great or small, are usually isolated from each other and surrounded by high, almost impassable mountains. In 1959, 30 of the capitals of the provinces of Peru had no road communication with the rest of the nation. It has always been that way.

The typical community is a little town of a few houses surrounding a square with a church, a municipal building, a jail, a few poorly stocked stores, and probably some unpaved streets. The doors of the houses are closed and no windows face the street. The life of the family goes on in the courtyards, where the few animals are kept and where flowers may be grown. The house, facing inward, is shut in on itself, and so is the town. The town is peaceful, quiet, self-conscious, and proud. Its contacts with the outside world are limited; it buys little and sells little. The capital of the state or of the nation is a long way off, and there is no reason for going there. Most of the things the town needs are locally produced. The houses are built of local materials, the shoes and clothing are locally made, and even now perhaps they are fashioned from hide locally tanned and cloth locally woven. Most of the food is grown nearby. If it is a large town of say 4,000 or 5,000 people, it will have a band and may even have a four-page weekly newspaper. A few of the more sophisticated residents may receive the big paper from the capital. The important institutions will be the town government, the school, and, most important of all, the church. These are the places where the whole town gathers.

But the community we have just described is relatively large. Most inhabited places are much smaller, with fewer than 400 people. Such a little village knows little of the nation and its politics. The police, the administrator appointed by the central government, and the echoes of an occasional political campaign are its only contacts with the outside world. It is almost as if the capital city and the rest of the country were in two different universes.

The capital city with its millions of human beings—Mexico, 2,500,000 for the city proper and 4,500,000 for the metropolitan district; Buenos Aires, 5,600,000 for the metropolitan district; the municipality of Rio de Janeiro, about 3,000,000; and Lima, over 1,000,000—belongs to a different world. The difference is not merely in size, although that is important. The case of Lima, the capital of Peru, is typical. It is not only the largest city; it is, one might say, the nation. It dominates all other towns. The next largest city is Arequipa with little over 100,000, followed by Trujillo with 50,000, Cuzco with another 50,000, Huancayo with 40,000, Ica 29,000, Piura 27,000, Cajamarca, where Atahualpa was strangled by Pizarro, 21,000, Puno 21,000, the recently expanded Chiclayo 45,000, and the Amazonian city of Iquitos about 42,000. That is all in a country of 10,000,000 people. The capital is larger than all of the other cities combined. This is also true of Mexico City, of Caracas in Venezuela, Santiago in Chile, Montevideo in Uruguay, and Buenos Aires in Argentina. It is true of the capitals of Central America and of the islands in the Caribbean.

Except for Brazil, Colombia, and Ecuador, which each have more than one large city, this is the case all over Latin America. And when one leaves the capital, one leaves the center of power, wealth, education, and the sophistication of the modern world. The gap between Lima and Cuzco, Trujillo, or Cajamarca is very wide. But the contrast between Lima and the thousands of little isolated towns hidden in mountain crevices is even greater.

Here is one of the basic dilemmas in Latin America. The little town of 100 or 200 families is the typical community. It is where the people live not only in Peru but in most of Latin America. If one excepts Argentina and Uruguay, 50 to 70 per cent or more of the people live in villages and plantations. They have almost nothing to identify them with the modern world. In Peru the villagers speak Quechua, not Spanish. They have no newspaper and there are no books, for the people are illiterate. There may be no school. The people go barefoot or wear homemade sandals. They sleep on the floor. They carry their burdens on their own backs. They have no modern tools and few animals. They have retained many of their ancient family customs, such as trial marriage. They may work their land in common, if they have any land at all. In look, manner, attitude, and belief, these Peruvians are not part of the same world as Lima. In any but a strictly legal sense, Lima is the capital only of itself and the nearby coastal region, but not of the mountains or the rest of the country. This is equally true of Guatemala City, and the list could be extended.

How different these two "worlds" may be is illustrated by the following incident. On a trip by automobile from Lima to Tingo María on the way toward the new port on the Ucayali River at Pucalpa, we passed an Indian plowing the land by the side of the road with an Incaic foot plow or *Tacla*, a pointed stick with a foot rest to push it into the ground. A woman and two children were helping him break the sod by turning it over with their hands after he had broken it with his ancient plow. Admittedly this is an extreme example, but after all it *was* along a modern automobile road. Admittedly too, my description of the Peruvian town is incomplete, but we are dealing with thousands of little towns that are not really a part of the same world as Lima. It is true that on the Peruvian coast the little towns are much closer to Lima. The people speak Spanish. They may have some modern tools and if they work on a plantation it is likely to be fully equipped with modern machinery. But the coast is not typical; most agriculture on the coast is under irrigation on large modern plantations.

The gap between the city and the country, between the large capital city and the provincial town, between the urban and the rural, is so wide that the people who live in one do not really understand those who live in the other. They live in different cultures even where, as in Colombia, they speak the same language. The isolation physically enforced by the mountains is intensified by an almost complete lack of communication between country folk and city dwellers.

The sophisticated university graduate whose eyes are turned toward Paris, who reads French, talks about dialectical materialism, psychoanalysis, and existentialism, has no language with which to converse meaningfully with the peasant who lives in a one-room hut with his wife and six children, even if the peasant does possess a limited Spanish vocabulary. The proverbial wisdom of the peasant and the sophisticated knowledge of the elite operate on two different planes and it is difficult for them to meet.

4. The Locality

There is, however, another side to this story. Isolation has given strength to localism, that is, a pride in the locality and its ways: Arequipa is "the mother of revolution," presidents of Venezuela come from Táchira, Sucre is the "real" capital of Bolivia, Cuzco is the "heart" of Peru. In this respect the government of Latin American nations has been controlled not by political parties but by regions, regional families, and regional *caudillos*. A political change has often meant merely that the people from one region have displaced those of another—that, for example, the Venezuelan *llanero* gives way to people from the *Sierra;* that Rio Grande do Sul replaces São Paulo in the government of Brazil; or that Guayquil rather than Quito is ruling Ecuador.

But localism is not only political. It is also social, racial, linguistic, and economic. In Brazil, Bahia's culture has many elements distinctively different from those of Rio Grande do Sul. Almost every part of Brazil is conscious of such differences. The language is filled with words, meanings, and accents that are local. In Mexico, the people of Yucatán, Tabasco, and Sonora are each equally proud of their own ways and scornful of the rest. In Colombia, Cartagena, Medellín, Cali, and Popayán are far different from Bogotá. In fact, the isolation imposed by almost impassable mountains has given a Colombian locality such as Tolima a sense of both cultural and political autonomy. The important influence has been the locality. And this is understandable enough. A place like Arequipa has been isolated from Lima throughout the centuries. To travel overland from one to the other until recently required about a month, for there were no roads and the mule paths were not made for speed or for a large army. To go by sea, from Arequipa to Mollendo on the coast, less than 100 miles away, was a three-day trek (before the railroads) and the rest of the trip to Lima would depend upon the good fortunes of a boat going north. In Brazil it was easier to go from Pará at the mouth of the Amazon to Europe than to Rio, and before airmail, a letter took a minimum of 40 days to reach Rio de Janeiro from Pôrto Velho on the upper Madeira River. The distance between Santa Cruz and La Paz in Bolivia is so great and, until the recently built modern highway, travel so difficult that there has long been a current of separatism in Santa Cruz.

From the east side of the *montaña* it seems natural to believe that the outlet is down the rivers to the Atlantic rather than through the jungle and over the Andes to the Pacific. Heavy freight from Iquitos, until a very few years ago, had to go down the Amazon for over 2,000 miles and then either round Cape Horn or go through the Panama

Canal to reach the capital of Peru, only 600 miles away as the crow flies. It can now go up the Ucayali River to Pucallpa and over the Andes on difficult roads to Lima.

To send freight from Cartagena to Bogotá is still something of a feat, as it is between Bluefields and Managua in Nicaragua, or between La Gran Savana and Caracas in Venezuela, for the link is by plane. In Colombia, there are many places that can only be reached by helicopter or on foot or horseback. If one remembers that these localities are not merely physical but in many instances linguistic, racial, and often economic "islands" as well, and that the capital is a different and perhaps hostile world, where provincial leaders have often been killed or exiled, and where manners, attitudes, and ways are so strange as to seem foreign, then the significance of this isolation becomes clear.

To contain these different universes within a single political framework is troublesome, but to forge a nation or develop a party system or a common ideal is even more difficult. *Caciquismo*—local bossism bent on looking after its own—with all of its innate possibilities for local tyranny and injustice, has at least one virtue—it *is* local. The people can identify with it against the center and follow the local leadership against the national government. Simply because he belongs to the locality, the local leader, no matter how repugnant he may seem to the "civilized," sophisticated, and educated in Mexico City, Bogotá, Caracas, or Lima, has the support of the locality. I am speaking not of the distant past but of the relatively recent days before airplane and military radio communication, when the center was much farther away and much less well informed, and when the locality and its leadership were not only a political but a military threat. Often the locality felt itself socially "superior" to the center and its leaders. As illustrated in Colombia in recent years, the natural difficulties of mountain, forest, and jungle can still make the locality confident of defending its interests and the center fearful and uncertain.

One could, of course, speak of the historic sectional attitudes of Texas, California, the South, and New England as illustrative of the point—except that one does not see the citizens of Texas marching on Washington to place a hero by force of arms in the presidential chair, either before or after an election. Yet exactly that has happened a thousand times in Latin America. The national energy and turbulence has come from the locality, the group, the region, the state. Moreover, this is only part of the meaning of internal isolation.

We must not look at countries like Mexico, Peru, or Guatemala as centralized governments with large capitals, surrounded by a number of smaller but comparable cities. In Peru, for instance, there are about 5,000 communes inhabited by an estimated 3,000,000 Indians who in many instances hold their lands in common and speak no Spanish. In rural areas, the majority live in groups located on plantations where the isolation from the outside world is very great indeed.

In Mexico there are over 100,000 neighborhoods, i.e., *pueblos, caseríos, ranchos*, etc., with an average size of less than 400 people. Every one of these communities is a self-contained world, separated, if not totally cut off, from the rest by a thousand different elements.

I remember on a market day standing in the doorway of a grocery store in one of the larger towns of Chiapas as the

Indians were coming into market, carrying their burdens on their backs. The owner of the store remarked as each one passed: "Tlajobal, . . . Chamula, . . . Matananguero."

"How do you know?" I asked.

"Oh, by their hats."

That was true. Each one that passed wore a different hat. He wore the hat of his community, and all the people in his village wore the same kind of hat. In Guatemala the village women wear blouses of distinctive color and design. Wherever she may go, each woman is recognized by the blouse she wears as belonging to a certain village.

Although these examples may be extreme, they are not unusual. Between thousands, if not tens of thousands, of communities—separated from each other by distance, difficult mountains, jungle, or desert—there are neither good roads nor always a common language (there are still about 90 languages recorded in Mexico). The census figures are, as Luis Alberto Sánchez says of statistics in Peru, poetry. Frequently there is hostility between the communities. They have different modes of dress, different kinds of housing, different family organization, and different skills. There are still elements of polygamy among the Chamula and Trique Indians in Mexico, for instance. Often each village has a separate craft—pottery, weaving, hammocks, sandals, firecrackers, burning charcoal, painted gourds, etc.

The individual who lives in one of these communities is related through extended family ties to almost every other member of the community. Not only are the families large and intermarried generation after generation, but the system of *compadrazgo* (godfather or godmother relationship) effectively binds the people together in such a way that in the smaller communities—and most of them are small—the individual is part of a beehive where the community acts, feels, and thinks as a single group. As one man said in explaining the difference between his and a neighboring village: "Say the children, say the women, say the men, says the whole village." The *pueblo* belongs to the individual and he to it.

These villagers do not migrate to other villages because they would be considered strangers, would have neither house nor land, neither family nor friends, and they would find the customs different. They might, in fact, not be allowed to stay. I have heard reports of cases within recent years of villages in Guatemala, Colombia, and Bolivia where strangers were encouraged to leave before nightfall.

This world lacks more than political integration. To be complete, the picture of separatism and localism has to take into account the hacienda, which occupies so large a place in the Latin American scene. The hacienda is almost completely autonomous, and its people seldom leave it. As late as 1923, in the State of Guanajuato in Mexico, 84 per cent of all the inhabited places were located on haciendas.

Notwithstanding the capital city with its centralization, the making of a nation has proved more difficult than the proclamation of nationalism as a credo and a policy. This is even true in Argentina.

The extensive cattle and sheep ranches in Argentina are merely a variation of this general pattern. Cattle ranches of 100,000 acres, and more, are common, and a single family may own a number of these in different parts of the country. A sheep farm may cover 1,000,000 or more acres. The population on the haciendas is small—a 50,000-acre cattle ranch may have only 200 workers on it, and a 1,000,000-acre sheep farm only a few more. The big house where the manager lives may have as many as 50 working people along with their wives and children. The rest will be scattered in small groups of 10 to 15, located many miles apart. The nearest ranch may be from 10 to 30 miles away and the nearest town more than 50 miles distant. Neighborliness, community, society, take on special meaning in this kind of a world.

The agricultural hacienda in Argentina is hardly less isolated than the cattle ranch. Although the hacienda may have a greater number of people per 1,000 acres, they live on separate plots of rented land. The rental arrangement usually requires the tenants to move every five years. The renter serves to improve the land for grazing, and then moves on.

As in other areas, the hacienda in Argentina is an isolating influence. In Argentina, however, the rural population is small, most people live in urban centers, and the owners of haciendas reside either in Buenos Aires or in Europe.

In Brazil the pattern of rural life is closer to that of the United States. The village or town tends to serve as a social center for the neighboring haciendas. The people from the fazendas (as haciendas are called in Brazil) will attend church in the central community, if it is not too far away. The owner and his family mounted and the *agregados* on foot will travel together. The town will also serve as a marketplace to which the *agregados* carry—usually on their heads—the few products they have to sell.

The children of the owner or administrator go to school

in the town, living in the house of their godparents. People from neighboring fazendas also come to town on special religious holidays and for the weddings and funerals of the owner's family, which become a kind of popular social function. If the neighboring fazendas are large enough to have their own chapels, they will be tended by the priest of the town church. It is also customary to make Sunday and holiday visits from the towns to the fazendas. But all of this is only true in the more populated areas where the towns have a settled neighborhood. There are many thousands of other settlements throughout Brazil, strung along river banks, on the shore of the ocean, or in forest clearings, where there is no contact with the larger world.

It must be remembered that in Brazil, as in most of Latin America, automobile roads are few and often impassable, and even the horse-drawn wagon, except in southern Brazil, is quite unknown. The usual means of transporting freight in southern Brazil, and in certain other limited areas like southern Colombia, is the oxcart. Everywhere else pack mules are usually driven over the trails. In the highlands of Peru and Bolivia llamas are used. Small boats and rafts carry freight along the streams and rivers, and over enormous areas in north and northeastern Brazil, and in the mountains of western South and Central America as well as in Mexico, freight is carried on the backs of human beings. It would be difficult to estimate the number of men and women who carry their goods from field to village or from home to market in this manner. The human carrier, in spite of the horse, the mule, the automobile, the railroad, and the airplane, is still a common sight, and in some areas is the usual means of carrying burdens long distances. This custom dies slowly, as anyone can testify who has gone by automobile from Mexico City to the market in Pachuca on a Friday when the fair is held there and has seen Indians with loads of pottery trotting along the road to town. Clearly isolation is still a major feature of rural life in Latin America.

CHAPTER 2

RACE

1. The Indian

IF ISOLATION is one of the keys to an understanding of
Latin America, the character of the Spanish conquest—as
distinguished from colonization or settlement—is another.
If by conquest we mean total submission to a conqueror, it
was never fully accomplished. In northern Mexico the
war against the Apaches went on into the late nineteenth
century; so, too, did the war against Indians in Argentina.
In Chile the Araucanians were not united with the republic until the middle of the last century. Even today
there are Indian groups not incorporated into the nation,
such as the Huichol in the high mountains of Nayarit in
Mexico, the Lacandon in the jungle of Chiapas, or the
Indians on the Upper Magdalena River in Colombia who
continuously war against the white men exploring for oil

or minerals. The Auca Indians in Ecuador recently murdered three white missionaries on the Napo River, and Brazilian Indians have in recent years attacked the parties stretching telegraph lines through the interior of the country. Many other small groups live beyond the formal rule of the state.

Conquest did not mean effective occupancy everywhere. The Spanish colonial government and society always had an unincorporated frontier which not even Jesuit or Franciscan missionaries could always penetrate successfully. Beyond this frontier neither the Spanish language nor the modern republican governments have fully established themselves, though the church has penetrated farther than other European institutions brought over by the conquerors.

But more important to the history and development of Latin America has been the failure of the Spanish crown to convert the American Indian into the ideal of a good European on the Spanish model. The Spanish conquest accomplished neither settlement, colonization, nor effective occupancy, but limited itself to military outposts, the gathering of tribute, the management of mines and ownership of plantations, dealing with the Indians only as government officials or as members of the church hierarchy.

The failure to colonize is understandable, and the Spanish achievement is still of heroic proportions. The terrain presented greater difficulties than in the United States, but that was of lesser importance than the presence of millions of human beings already on the land. The surprise of the European at the variety of peoples and cultures and their incredible, almost enchanted forms—as if they were of another world and especially molded to serve the devil, as many of the Spaniards believed—could not have been greater than the surprise of the Indians. For to the Indians the Spaniards were creatures from Heaven, veritable gods possessed of magical powers. Between these two races no effective means of understanding, no moral basis of accommodation was ever found. They met as billiard balls do on a billiard table. They met but did not penetrate. The one exception was the Catholic mission. It was only there that the Indian prospered and multiplied. Everywhere else he was troubled by mistreatment, and perhaps most of all, by the strange ways and expectancies of his conquerors. The missions, however, had a marginal role in the total enterprise and an unhappy ending.

The rest of the story of the relations between the European and the Indian has been one of incessant attrition. The Indian proved stubborn and unyielding, while Spanish colonial policies in some measure insulated the Indian from the disintegrating influences of the conquistador and his heirs.

The complicated history of colonial legislation and administration cannot be considered here, but it is sufficient to say that wherever the Indian managed to retain his land and his own community, he remained an Indian, keeping his language, his customs, his family organization, his religious rituals even if he became a Catholic, using the same tools, working the land much the same way as before the conquest, eating the same food and living in the same kind of house. The Spanish influence was important enough. It deprived the Indian of his leadership, of his learned men, of his old idols and old priests, of his men of science, of his government, and of his faith in himself as a man. It imposed upon him tribute, services, and demands for labor which proved damaging and led to a decline in the Indian population during the colonial period. Letters of the viceroys of Peru are filled with repeated prognostications that the Indian *"se está acabando"* (is disappearing).

But when he survived and lived in his own community, he remained an Indian in his ways and attitudes. When the Indian community was incorporated into a hacienda, where it retained some of its community organization and collective responsibilities, Indian characteristics could also survive, although to a lesser degree. Only when the natives were drawn into the urban centers, into mining towns, and into cities as servants and workers, learning European skills, did they cease to be Indians.

The Spanish conquest found in the Indian population a barrier which it never fully overcame. A cultural community is more resilient than a forest. The American pioneer could fell his trees and clear his lands, because on the whole the country was empty. In Latin America all of the seemingly occupiable land was already filled, and the people on it continued to till it as they had before. Now they worked the land of a European master, or paid tribute to him, but they continued to be Indians in their language and ways. They refused to learn to be good Europeans, even if they were beaten or had their ears cut off. They obeyed their new masters because they had no choice. They did his services but nothing more. Withdrawn and silent, with bowed head, they made no claims on anyone, except, if possible, to be left alone. The result was a nation within a nation, a culture within a culture, two people living in proximity but belonging to two different universes.

A contemporary Ecuadorian historian describes what happened to the Indian in the following words: "The psychological resistance of the Indian to the Spaniard was and remains to this day, in his repugnance to the assimilation of the white man's civilization, one of the most extraordinary phenomenon in human history. This resistance has lasted for ages and has the frightening implication of collective suicide." (Alfredo Pareja y Diezcanseco: *Historia del Ecuador,* 1938, Vol. I, p. 222.)

This is not the entire story. There were notable exceptions. But the Spanish conquest did not change the Indian into a good European on the Spanish model nor has he become a good Latin American. Anyone who will take the trouble can see this today easily in Guatemala.

The Guatemalan Indian in Chichicastenango, or in San Miguel Acatlan, is not a white man, does not want to be one, and disciplines those of his members who are too friendly or try to ape white men. A few white men govern and collect taxes and exploit the Indians as they can. But there is no friendship between them, no understanding, and in spite of proximity, in spite of the fact that both the Indian and the *Ladino* (white man) have taken certain cultural traits from each other—like the tortilla on one side and the European chicken or sheep on the other— they do not intermingle socially, they do not intermarry. Whatever process of amalgamation ever took place between the two races has, in Indian areas today, probably declined.

Yet the Indian population is in all probability increasing

more rapidly than the more urbanized population. In Peru, Ecuador, and Bolivia, the Indian is in the majority—regardless of what the official statistics say. The statistics, to repeat Luis Alberto Sánchez, are poetry. And this problem of the Indian in varying degrees is well-nigh universal. It was eliminated in Argentina in 1879 by a process of what can only be described as extermination under a military campaign by General Julio A. Roca. In Uruguay and Costa Rica it is practically non-existent. But in most of the continental countries there are smaller or larger groups that do not identify with the ruling elements of the nation or in fact with the nation itself.

General Cárdenas expressed this one day after a visit to the Yaqui Indians—"*Somos extrangeros aquí*" (We are foreigners here).

When one asks for an explanation of the difficulties in any one of the Andean countries, or in Central America and Mexico, one of the answers is that they are not homogeneous nations. No one knows how many Indians there are in Latin America. Figures that have been given vary between 14,000,000 and 30,000,000. It depends upon the definition of who is an Indian. If an Indian who learns to say a few words in Spanish is no longer counted an Indian, you get one result. If race rather than language is used, then you get another. The point to remember is that the population in Latin America has doubled in the last 30 years, and the Indian population has also doubled.

In failing to integrate the Indian, Spain also failed to make the Spanish language the universal medium of communication. It was a very great achievement to have spread the Castillian tongue over so vast an area and to

have made it possible for the people in Chile to feel at
home in the language spoken in Mexico. But this achievement again has fallen short of its ideal aim. The Indian
does not speak Spanish, or if he has picked up some Spanish words, he does not use them at home. The women
usually know less of the white man's language than do the
men, and the farther we go from the big city, the provincial capital, the county seat, the less frequently is Spanish
the language of the people.

In Mexico the Summer Institute of Linguistics is now
working with 77 languages and is aware of at least 12
more which it is not studying. Even some large cities are
bilingual, meaning, usually, that the European has
learned to speak the native tongue. These larger cities are
Mérida, Asunción, Cuzco, and Santiago de Estero. Of
course, many of the provincial capitals and municipal
(county) centers are bilingual. Theaters in Indian tongue
are still in existence in Mérida (Maya) and Asunción
(Guarani).

From my knowledge of the area and the people I would
guess that there are no accurate figures of the number of
Chamula or Trique Indians and certainly no accurate
count of how many of them speak Spanish. This is also
true of other places where Indians are numerous. The
inadequate reach of the Spanish tongue is illustrated by
the necessity for whites and mestizos to learn the language
of the Indians in places where they abound. In Yucatán
the whites speak Maya; in Paraguay the entire population
is said to be bilingual, speaking Guarani as well as Spanish. Most of the mestizos in Ecuador, Peru, and Bolivia
who live outside of the capital speak Aymara or Quechua.

In Guatemala those whites who have permanent residence in the rural districts or provincial towns know the local language.

We really have no adequate picture of the effective reach of Spanish and therefore no real understanding of the political, social, and cultural difficulties that face these nations. Our preoccupation with the big city and its many offshoots has blinded North and South Americans to the complexity of the culture south of the United States.

That culture is not only Latin but also American—and American means Indian, and Indian means non-European not only in race and language but in a thousand other things as well. That the Latin will ultimately absorb the American has been taken for granted from the beginning, more than four centuries ago. And so it may prove in the end, but the end is a long way off and history has shown itself capable of many an unexpected turn. The idea of the Quechua nation, a resuscitation of an older Incaic pattern, is not beyond possibility, and the spread of literacy may have consequences other than those its advocates dream of.

2. The Mestizo

This brings us to the mestizo. The mestizo, the child of a European father and an Indian mother, is the most important by-product of the Spanish conquest. This child of Europe and America has taken over the leadership of Latin America. The president of the country, the members of the cabinet, the general of the army, the artist like Diego Rivera, the novelist like Ciro Alegría or Machado de Assis, the politician, businessman, university professor, is likely to be a mestizo. While Argentina, Uruguay, and central Chile are classified as white, the important European immigration to these countries came after the middle of the nineteenth century. Until then the population was predominantly mestizo, and the mixed strain has not entirely disappeared. And as one goes from Buenos Aires to Tucumán, Salta, and Jujuy, the Indian strain becomes more and more evident. Generally speaking, where the Indian has disappeared or declined in numbers, the mestizo, the Negro, and the mulatto—and not the European—have taken his place.

It is, I think, safe to say that the mestizo is the dominant influence in Latin America. This is a remarkable achievement. For the mestizo is a new race, nonexistent at the time of the discovery and looked upon with suspicion and hostility throughout the three centuries of colonial rule. The colonial governments, the Spaniards, and the *criollos* treated the mestizo as an inferior human being, described him as undependable, as possessing the bad characteristics of the Spaniard and Indian, as lazy, a vagabond, unstable and untrustworthy. And, in fact, more than one Latin American sociologist, as for instance Carlos Octavio Bunge, in the early part of this century ascribed Latin America's political and social shortcomings to the racial hybrid and saw little hope for the future. They repeated the estimate of the Spanish viceroys who deplored the presence of the mestizo as a disturbing element, difficult to discipline.

Whatever the objective merits of this judgment, the fact remains that the mestizo came into the world, usually outside the marriage bond—though in the days of the conquest, there were also some notable cases of marriage between conquistadors and Incaic "princesses" in Peru—was abandoned by his father and raised by his mother, and was neither Indian nor Spaniard. He grew up in a world of unstable values, where his mother and father lived in different cultures, had different standards of conduct, different notions of good and right, and different basic loyalties. He had no tradition, no invariable rules, no place in the community comparable with his ambitions. While the Indian wished only to be left alone in his little village, the mestizo aspired to the place of his father, the European, the *criollo*. The wars of independence gave him his first opportunity to play a role on the public scene and gave him a footing on the social and economic ladder. The mestizo was the soldier, the corporal and sergeant, the subordinate official. It was only after the wars—during which the chief leaders were *criollos*—that the mestizo began to rise from the lower ranks to colonel and general.

The turbulence and the civil wars that tore apart Latin America for a century provided the mestizo with the opportunity to assert his leadership. A glance at the figures who played the major political roles before 1850 and after is revealing. By mid-century the mestizo had established his dominance in government and politics, had risen in social status, repudiated his Indian heritage, and taken over *criollo* and European ways. The turbulence, the instability, is in one sense both the evidence and the means of the change that took place in this child of two races. Where he reached for status and wealth he did so largely, however, at the expense of the Indian and at the price of increasing the gap that separates the Indian from his rulers.

The so-called liberal revolutions in Mexico, Guatemala,

Ecuador, and generally throughout Latin America ended with the defeat of the *criollo* oligarchy that had survived the independence, stripped the church of its lands, and endowed the mestizo with worldy power. He became the master of the Indian and the owner of land. He acquired property taken from the church, and now, as general, governor, cacique, and president, married into the older oligarchy. The liberal revolutions of the 1850's and later—the one in Guatemala in 1871, for example—tended to give the Indian equality before the law but did not change his social status or increase his economic opportunities, and, as in Mexico, weakened his ability to defend his communal lands against the expanding hacienda. These changes did not bring the Indian and mestizo closer together. In fact, it increased the distance between them, and the mestizo joined the *criollo* in viewing the Indian as an inferior being. So that now, as one American anthropologist has said of a certain part of Guatemala, it is "completely improbable" for a marriage between an Indian and a mestizo to take place. This statement for a particular community in Guatemala can be generalized for the Indian areas as a whole. The Indian, to achieve social status among mestizos, must first shed his language, his clothes, his ways, his occupation, his family, and his community—a difficult venture at best.

3. The Negro

The Negro, like the Indian and the mestizo, has a special place and a unique role in the Latin American complex. Of the 12,000,000 or more Negroes transported by slave traders to the Western Hemisphere between 1500 and 1850, a large proportion went to what are now the Latin American nations. In greater or lesser numbers they were to be found in every part of the area from Chile to Cuba. Next to Haiti, the largest proportion probably went to Brazil, although Cuba was a close third. There are certain general features of the Negro's role in Latin America which have influenced both the economic and the social development of the area. For one thing, in those regions where the Indian disappeared shortly after European conquest, or proved too intractable, Negro labor was used instead. Generally the Negro did not play an important part in those areas where the Indian survived in large numbers—usually settled agricultural regions. The Negro survived and prospered best in tropical parts of America, largely the coastal lowlands. As a laborer he was employed mainly in the cultivation of sugar, cocoa, and other crops that do well in warm moist climates.

The Negroes were purchased as *individuals* by European masters and were therefore closer to and more dependent on the white man. In fact, some Negroes arrived with the early Spanish expeditions. Although they were slaves, they were treated in some ways as superior to the Indian and were used occasionally as foremen or overseers where Negro and Indian labor were found together. Unlike the Indian, who has proved extremely recalcitrant, the Negro was malleable and culturally receptive. He acquired European language, religion, dress, food, and habits with surprising speed, and in those countries where he is numerically important, he has become a significant influence in the economic, political, and, especially, in the cultural life. He has, as the Indian has not, become culturally a European, and in Brazil, Cuba, Venezuela, and Panama won recognition in literature, music, art, and architecture. This has notably been the case in Brazil where some of the greatest figures in the arts, music, and literature have been mulattoes and Negroes.

It is interesting to speculate on the significance of this remarkable turn of events. The slave, branded and chained, has within a relatively short period of time become one of the leading cultural influences among his former masters. Even while slavery was still in existence (it was abolished in Cuba in 1890 and in Brazil in 1888) the mulatto everywhere identified with the Negro either as slave or as a free man, and the Abolitionist movement in Brazil was to a large extent carried on by mulattoes and by freed slaves.

Unlike the Indian, the Negro found leaders among members of his own race. More than that, he become identified with and sometimes a distinguished participant in the general culture without relinquishing his Negro heritage, whereas among the Indians, neither the mestizo nor even the pure Indian, such as Juárez, who became president of Mexico, identified with the Indian or defended him against the white man.

The Indian had no natural and trusted spokesman of his own race and no interpreter acceptable to the larger community, whereas the Negro had many. The Negro felt at home in some subtle sense even while he was a slave—as the reading of the literature will reveal. The Indian never felt at home with the white man and does not today. But there are other historical influences which help explain the accommodation of the Negro within the Latin American community in a way that has not happened in the United States.

The Negro slave, brought into the Iberian peninsula as early as 1442, fitted into a society where slavery was still in existence. As a result of the many centuries of warfare with the Moors, if not for other reasons, Spanish society accepted slavery as normal, while it had long since died out in Western Europe. At the time the Negro was brought to Spain, there were Moorish slaves, Jewish slaves, and even some native Spaniards were slaves. Captured prisoners could be held for ransom or could be held as slaves, and the laws allowed other reasons for slavery. But the important point is that there was a slave law, an elaborate code, embodied as part of the *Siete Partidas* going back to Alfonso the Wise (1252–84), which endowed the slave with a legal personality, with duties, and with rights. The slave was known to the law as a human being; he could marry, he could buy his freedom, he could change his master if he found one to purchase him, and he could under certain conditions testify in court even against his master. If a slave became a priest, he had to give his master one slave, but if he became a bishop, he had to give him two slaves.

The Negro brought over from Africa became the beneficiary of this body of law. He was not merely a slave—a chattel, as he was under West Indian and American colonial codes—but also a human being with rights enforceable in the king's court. The Negro in Iberia was also converted to the Catholic faith, and the master had to see to it that he came to church. While Catholic doctrine did not oppose slavery as such, it asserted that master and slave were equal in the sight of God, that what mattered was the moral and religious character of man, and that the master must treat his slaves as moral beings, as brothers in

Christ. It also emphasized the merits of manumission. Negroes in Spanish and Portuguese colonies were the inheritors of this legal and religious tradition. It is not suggested that slavery was not cruel, nor that in Brazil, Cuba, Venezuela, or Peru abominable and inhuman acts were not committed against Negro slaves. But cruelty was against the law, and unusual punishment could be brought to the attention of the court by a recognized legal protector of the slave. The killing of a slave was treated as murder. The entire atmosphere was different, and manumission was so frequent that there were often more freed Negroes than there were slaves.

The fact that the slave had both a legal personality and a moral status made manumission natural and the abolition of slavery no great shock. The question of the slave's fitness for freedom never arose, and the freed Negro was a free man, not a freedman. He was legally the equal of all other free men. And when slavery was abolished in Brazil, the crowd in the galleries threw flowers upon the members of the Congress, and the people danced in the streets of Rio de Janeiro throughout the night. The question of segregation, so agonizing and so disturbing in our own South, could never have arisen anywhere in Latin America —neither with the Negro nor with the Indian. It is this tradition in Latin America that makes it most difficult for them to understand our problem or our way of dealing with it.

4. Racial Prejudice

This does not mean there is no racial prejudice in Latin America. It exists against both the Indian and the Negro, but it is a prejudice which has no sanction in the law. It is social and economic and cultural. It is determined more by social status than by a sense that people of color are inferior in nature—though this feeling exists, particularly regarding the Indian. But any Indian, and any mulatto, if he can escape from his poverty, if he can acquire the graces, the language, the manners, the dress, the schooling, and the associations that will admit him into the best society, will have no insuperable difficulties socially, especially if he is wealthy, and can, if he has it in him, be elected to Congress, be a member of the cabinet, or become president of the country. The fact that he is an Indian or a mulatto will not bar him—and there are some instances of mulattoes and a few Indians who have risen to the highest posts politically. In that sense there is no race prejudice. The case is different for the pure black man. In some countries—in Peru for instance, or Ecuador, Colombia, or Venezuela, or perhaps even in Cuba and Brazil—the pure black man so far has not and perhaps cannot rise to the highest political post or really be accepted by the "best" social set. That is the difference between Latin American racial conditions and our own.

I have probably overdrawn the picture. The tolerance is very great, but not absolute. In Cuba, which certainly is as broadly open as any country in Latin America, the numerous social clubs were exclusively white (before Castro); the fact that a Negro rebellion in which 3,000 lost their lives was possible as late as 1911 casts a long shadow on the white-colored complex in that country. In Panama where the Negroes have assimilated into the Spanish tradition, they identify with the middle class and look down upon the thousands of Negroes brought over from the

British West Indies during the construction of the Panama Canal. When a Panamanian speaks of the Negro in Panama, these are the people he refers to. Other illustrations could be added, but it remains true that Latin American attitudes toward the Negro are of a different quality than our own.

There is something else that needs adding. In the United States the Negro's opportunities for wealth, education, professional advancement as doctor or lawyer, and for active politics (outside of the South) are very much greater than in Latin America. True enough, this advancement economically and professionally takes place mostly, though by no means entirely, within the colored community. But the way is not closed—in the arts, in the professions, in education, or in opportunities for distinction. The road is narrow and steep, but there is a road. In contrast, in Latin America the road does not exist. This is too strong a way to put it. Perhaps it would be more accurate to say that the door is shut but not locked. The gap between the "lower" classes—between not only the Indian and the Negro poor, but all the poor, all the illiterate, and all the children of the little rural hut that I saw in Cundinamarka—and the elite in Bogotá, or between the *huasipongo* on a hacienda in Ecuador and the traveled, sophisticated literary people in Quito is so wide that it is almost unbridgeable. That is, in part, because the countries are poor, the wealthy families fewer, and the indigent more numerous.

But there is a more important point. The hierarchical structure of the society, the aristocratic tradition, the essentially castelike way people are grouped and identified, and the paternal concept that the poor must always be poor, that the servant must always remain a servant, has made the gap between "upper" and "lower" very great indeed. Never in the history of the United States has there been such a distance, such a seemingly impossible distance, between our poorest farmer or immigrant and the wealthiest and most self-conscious of our aristocracy—if that word has any real meaning in our culture. This distance is obviously not racial, not biological, nor based on color of skin or place of origin, but it is perhaps even more effective as a dividing line, and perhaps more permanent. It is an ingrained part of the total scheme of things.

We are fooling ourselves—and Latin Americans who speak as if this were not the case are also fooling themselves—if we or they think that what we call democracy is a thing of formal law and constitutional enactment. It has as a background a feeling of equality, or perhaps egalitarianism, "where a man is a man for all that," where no man rides a high horse and is not expected to ride one. At this point American and Latin American society stand wide apart. The difference between the basic conditions of social equality and opportunity in the United States and Latin America is broad and deep—and not really changeable for a long time to come.

CHAPTER 3

RELIGION

1. The Church in the Colony

AT THE TIME of the discovery the American Indian was a profoundly religious and mystical human being. A great part of his daily existence was bound up in religious rites, in propitiating his many gods, in finding grace, justification, and peace. Every act had its religious significance, every wind, every change in the color of the moon, every appearance of the unexpected, had its religious portent. In such highly developed cultures as the Aztec and the Inca, a large priesthood served to interpret the will of the gods. A mystical philosophy, a questioning of the essence of human existence, informed and disciplined the attitude of the Indian toward life and death.

The Spanish conquest was indifferent to the spiritual and moral values that ruled the lives of the American Indians. The conquistador, whatever his virtues of courage and fealty, was no philosopher, no mystic, and oblivious—in most cases—to the meaning of the strange world in which he found himself.

The greatest shock to American Indian civilization was the complete denial of its existence by the soldiers of Spain, a denial manifest in indifference to or in deliberate destruction of the Indians' ancient gods, their objects of worship, and their temples. Pulling the gold off the walls in the Temple to the Sun in Cuzco was merely one of a thousand instances of irreverence for the spirit of a culture that was centered in religion. In destroying the religious temples and the religious leaders, the conquistadors also destroyed the soul of Indian civilization. Its values, its beliefs, its pattern of existence, its great art and artists were scattered by the wind that blew across the ocean.

What was left of the Indian as a spiritual human being, whose belief in God was burdened by the sudden tragedy that had overtaken his world, found refuge in the Christian Church. That is the true meaning of the conversion of millions of Indians in so short a time. After everything had been taken from the Indian by men he could not understand, whose motives were completely incomprehensible to him, the Catholic Church saved what meaning there was left to existence. In the Church the Indian could rebuild his faith in the forces that govern the world, that bring day and night, sunshine and rain, life and death. The Church wisely built where the old temples were, and the saints of the Church gave the Indian full scope for his attachment to a particular mystery, a special symbol, a unique identity with forces that lay beyond human reach and were all-powerful. The Church did something in addition. Bringing the conqueror and the conquered into the same fold, it gave the Indian identity with the European and a sense that they were both mortal. It gave the conquistador a conscience, the sense that he was dealing with human beings who had souls, who were inside of his Church and children of the same God as himself. But it required a Papal Bull to make that point for the conquistador. The strangeness of American culture, the ways of the Indians, the bitterness of the conquest, and the belief in the devil working his evil designs through strange beings made it easy for the conquistador to deny the Indian's claim to human fellowship.

The cry of Las Casas (the Bishop of Guatemala whose lifelong defense of the Indians took him across the Atlantic more than a dozen times) that "all men are men and nothing more" was a denial that the conquistador was different or by nature better than the Indian. His assertion to Charles V, before whom he was pleading for justice to the Indians, that "he would not go across the room to serve the King unless it was also to save the King's conscience" was a courageous reminder to a Catholic king that his ultimate reward was to be had only from the hand of God, that though he was king, the reward would be withheld if he failed to earn it by doing justice on this earth.

The Church was the Indian's salvation here and now by giving him a place where he could feel free in spirit and where he could reweave the threads that had always bound him to the world beyond his immediate senses. This is a service that the Church has continued to perform for the Indian, even though in subsequent centuries the particular zeal of the early friars has not been equaled, and problems of a political and social nature have arisen. But these are secondary to the great spiritual role the Church has played in the life of the Indian.

In the centuries following the conquest, the Church grew in influence, power, and wealth. Its missions to the Indians at the outer edge of the settled areas and beyond the political dominion of the state served to bring the most distant and culturally isolated groups into contact with European ideas regarding Church and state. Under Franciscan and Jesuit auspices, a series of communal villages prospered and flourished until the expulsion of the Order of Jesus in 1767 and the destruction of the Franciscan missions during the wars of independence. It is important to repeat that the only contact with Europeans not unkindly to the American Indian was through the mission. The nonmaterial, the mystical, and in some sense the impersonal character of primitive Indian religion found the nonindividualistic, impersonal, and communal bent of the religious orders congenial to their own sense of the order of things. In the mission they multiplied and prospered, and the disappearance of the mission meant the passing of the only friend the Indian had, either in South or North America. Missions to the Indians have returned intermittently here and there since the independence, but they are few, insecure, and apprehensive of a sudden change in political mood which will drive them once again from their labors. The modern temper is not congenial to the missions, and, for lack of another political issue, they provide a good excuse for political agitation.

It is useful in trying to unravel the mysteries of Latin American culture to remember that under the colonial system the Church ruled while the state governed. The state

in its paternal preoccupation dealt with the public and
material aspects of life, but the Church ruled the most intimate and personal needs of the individual, from the cradle
to the grave and beyond. The Church in the large city, in
the small town, in the village, and even on the pathways
over the mountains was ever-present, for there would be a
cross or small chapel at every difficult passage, at the top
of every hill one climbed. The Church was everywhere—
even when the priest was absent. But so it had been before the conquest and before the white man. Every mountain, every stream, every strange and marvelous thing
contained some symbol of the forces beyond man's reach,
and to the unpretentious, the humble, and the pious, simple things are marvelous and strange. Each location had
its own *huaco*. In the new faith the *huaco* (the spirit of the
place) became a favorite and miraculous saint.

The Church was everywhere and with every individual
all of his life. The day began with early morning mass and
ended with an Ave Maria, and every occasion, every sorrow, every joy, every holiday, had its own special religious
symbolism to be acted out in church. During the colonial
period the Church was also the school, the university, the
hospital, the home of the aged, the sick, and the abandoned. It served the individual and the community in
many ways.

In the absence of newspapers, libraries, museums, and
theaters, the religious ritual of the churches, the orders,
the monasteries, and the convents gave the individual a
place in an enchanted and meaningful world. Everything
that happened, from a bullfight to the arrival of a new
viceroy, an earthquake, or the king's birthday, always involved public ceremony. The processions, prayers, masses,

and sermons in which the Church participated made it perhaps the chief actor in the drama or, better, the chief embodiment of the symbolism that endowed every activity with meaning. It surrounded life at all turns and all times. The church or cathedral bell dominated the community, and daily life was regulated by its sound. In a world that had settled down to quietude, isolation, and a preoccupation with status and place, in a world where there was no real adventure, no honors to be won, no public posts or responsibilities to be acquired (for the native *criollo* was generally denied public office), where travel was difficult and required permission—where social dignities were composed of such minutiae as where one had a right to sit in church, in which aisle, on what side of what official, or how many steps behind, of whether one had a right to carry a sword or to claim a title—in that kind of a world the Church was a great solace and a great spectacle at the same time.

In a city like Lima, Quito, or Mexico City, the Church buildings and monasteries dominated the scene, and the profession of priest or membership in an Order, a monastery, or a convent was a high calling and a privilege. The few diaries that have come down from the colonial period reveal preoccupation with the ever-present Church. The daily record is filled with religious processions, with the celebration of the saint's day in this or that monastery, church, convent, or ward, with gossip, scandal, and even public riots over the election of a prior or prioress in a monastery or convent.

Riva Agüero, the famous Peruvian historian, speaks of colonial Lima as a "conventual city." Latin America was so far away from Europe, from the king and the court, from the excitement of European wars and marching troops, that Europe and its doings were illusive, and all political pretension to honor, glory, and knighthood (which could be purchased) were also unreal. But the Church was here-and-now and had room for every member of the society, from the poor Negro slaves and Indians to the *criollo* aristocrats who were descended from the conquistadors and filled with a pride consistent with their own self-esteem. In the Church they each had a niche and they each had a special corner, a favorite saint, a special *cofradía*. When all of the churches, monasteries, and convents took part in a solemn procession with the military, the viceroy, the Audiencia, the city fathers (the *cabildo*), and the Church dignitaries, the result was a colorful and solemn occasion that attracted everyone in the city and gave each individual an opportunity to take pride in his own favorite saint, or in that of his parish, his *cofradía,* his church, his order. Clearly enough, the Church filled the life of the community, for there was in fact no other institution that embraced all the people regardless of race, color, poverty, sickness or wealth, age or youth.

The Church was also wealthy, powerful, and conscious of its prerogative. The difference between the claims of the Church and the state during the colonial period were modulated by the king, who was also the patron of the Church. Pope Alexander VI had given to the Spanish kings the patronage of the Church for their support in the conversion of the Indians and their aid to the Church. In time, however, the *patronato* came to mean a claim of control over the Church, so as to make it subordinate to the civil power. Thereafter, the Church had no freedom, either to build a cathedral, lay out a parish, nominate a priest to a country church, collect the tithes, or publish a Papal Bull without the consent of the king. All of the great power of the Church, all of its great wealth, were confined within the jurisdiction of the crown, and when Charles III expelled the Order of Jesus from his American colonies, he did so without giving the Order any notice and without offering any explanation.

2. The Church After Independence

The independence movement brought so many difficulties to the Church that it has not to this day fully recovered from them. For one thing, the Church dignitaries, being mainly Spanish, were less friendly to the independence movement than the lower clergy.

The lower clergy, in fact, played an important role in the independence movement. Father Miguel Hidalgo y Costilla and Father José María Morelos were the great leaders of the rebellion in Mexico. Hidalgo occupies in Mexico a place similar to that of Washington in the United States. In Uruguay, two priests accompanied the gauchos led by José Gervasio Artigas and fought by their side with lance in hand against the Spaniards. The clergy, the poorer members of the hierarchy, disobeyed their bishops and identified themselves with the movement. Father Pérez Castellano wrote the Bishop of Buenos Aires that he could not for the moment appear before his court to answer charges against him because he was busy with his duties as a member of the local junta in Montevideo, duties which the Archbishop declared incompatible with the obligations of a priest. This division within the Church persisted throughout the greater part of the struggle against Spain.

As a result, the American churches operated to a considerable extent without bishops during, and for a period after, the conflict. And during the conflict the Papacy sided with Spain against the independence movement—among other reasons because of the pressure of the powerful Spanish Embassy in Rome. After all, Spain had been the great defender of the faith since the Reformation. Against the ideas of the French revolution, which were known and proclaimed by the fighters for independence in Latin America, the continuance of Spanish sovereignty seemed to the Church on the side of justice, morality, and faith.

The resulting rift between the American leadership and Rome was aggravated by the new governments' claim to the rights of the *patronato* which had been exercised by the Spanish crown, and by the insistence of the Church that the patronage had been personal with the king, and now that the king was gone from America, the Church was free. This question remains in fact unsettled and variously compromised in different countries.

More serious, perhaps, than this was the struggle that emerged between Church and state when the new governments attempted to pattern themselves on French and American constitutional precepts. It became quickly evident that the modern state—with its efforts to control education, to enforce the same law equally against all citizens, and to oppose corporate privileges, i.e., *fueros* (special laws enforceable in ecclesiastical courts) and exemption from taxation for Church properties—meant trouble for the Church. In fact, the revolutionary lawyers, trained in Roman Law and imbued with French anti-clericalism on one side, and the priests, traditionally identified with the corporate Church and its claims on the individual on the other, found it most difficult to abide in the same world. The quarrel between the anti-clerical lawyer, steeped in concepts of absolute sovereignty, and the priest, who looked upon all matters that might touch the soul and affect human salvation as the special responsibility of the Church, ended in a conflict that was often bitter and bloody. The lawyer won the battle. The Church in most countries lost its land, its wealth, its monopoly over education, its censorship over literature and the press, its control over the hospitals, over public charity, over the universities, over marriage (for civil marriage became legal), over the registration of birth, over the burial grounds, and over the right to exclude other faiths from the country. The Church came out of the struggle much poorer, much less influential, and in most places on the defensive against continuing threats to its remaining power.

A hundred years of conflict has gradually attenuated the bitterness, and the Church has recently recovered a measure of prestige by taking sides against the dictatorship of Perón in Argentina, Rojas Pinilla in Colombia, Pérez Jiménez in Venezuela, less openly against Batista in Cuba, and, most recently, against Trujillo in Santo Domingo.

It has also taken a definite position on behalf of land reform and has slowly come to voice the social doctrines expressed in the *Rerum Novarum* of Pope Leo XIII. In some measure, excepting the present troubles in Cuba, the Church's political position is better than it has been since the break with Spain. It is more independent of the state and perhaps closer to the social movement sweeping Latin America than it was a few years ago. But these changes vis-à-vis the state and public policy have had little to do with the role of the Church as a religious institution. The people have remained Catholic and the Latin American who professes anti-clericalism often is married in church, dies in the faith, and his children are baptized as if he had never fallen under the influence of the French philosophers of the eighteenth century or the Marxists of the nineteenth and twentieth centuries.

3. The Role of the Church

The role of the Church in Latin America is different from what it is in the United States. The city, the town, the village, the *barrio,* has its patron or patroness—Santa Rosa in Lima, the Virgin of Guadalupe in Mexico, etc. Every parish in turn has a saint of its own—St. Francis, St. Dominic, St. John. Every guild—the goldsmiths, the seamen, the carpenters—used to have its own saint, with its own *cofradía* inside the church, its own chapel in a corner. Every large hacienda had, and mostly still has, a chapel or sometimes a church, which occasionally connects with the main house, so that one goes from one part of the house to the other by passing through the chapel. This chapel has its own saint who in some intimate way belongs to the family. He is the family patron who looks after its members and protects them. His name is invoked on every occasion. He has a familiar presence in family affairs, as if he were a living member of it. The children are baptized and married in the family chapel and in the presence of the family patron, and in this chapel the members of the family used to be buried. The patron of the family is also the patron of the plantation community. The entire life of the plantation community is lived and in some measure ordered by the sound of the chapel bell. This is true of the smaller towns, the smaller cities, and to some extent of the larger ones.

Less than 100 years ago, travelers told ои the cathedral bells in Quito ringing for vespers, the entire city becoming quiet, the people kneeling down in the streets, taking off their hats, and saying their prayers. To a degree it is still true, more of the women than of the men, more of the unsophisticated, the poor, the illiterate, than others. It is true for the country folk and even more so for the Indians.

This sense of intimacy with the mysteries and meaning of the Church is seen in the family in another way. Each member, old or young, has a patron saint. The big occasion is not the child's birthday but the Saint's day after whom the child was named—St. Francis, St. John, St. Peter. The day is like Christmas. It begins with going to mass accompanied by one's friends all in their best clothes. All through the day there are presents, music, and visits, and sometimes the dancing goes on late into the night. And as the families are large, there are numerous occasions for such festivities. Each member of the family —the grandparents, the parents, the children, and the grandchildren—has his own particular patron saint whose day is celebrated in similar fashion. Then there are the numerous first, second, third, and fourth cousins, the aunts and uncles, the school friends, the companions and associates in business or in the professions, and last but not least, the *compadres*—the godfathers and godchildren —who may literally run into the dozens.

Thus the life of the family and of the individual is greatly and continuously involved with the Church. One must not exaggerate the implications of this relationship of the individual, the family, and the community to the Church. But one should also be careful not to underestimate it. It gives life a certain quality and adds something to the meaning of daily activities which is lacking in the United States. In Latin America going to church is not just a Sunday affair. The priest and the bishop are present on every important occasion. There are few gatherings of intellectuals where some member of a religious order does not take an active part. And there are certainly few public affairs where the members of the Church are not active participants. This participation is uneven and varies with the community, but where it occurs there is always added colorfulness and solemnity. On even the least religious occasions, a certain emphasis upon eternal verities is added by the presence of Franciscan or Dominican brothers, or when the Bishop of Ibara takes part in a conference on history and illustrates a point in popular folklore by playing the song on a piano. The Church is an active part of the daily life of both the individual and the community, and its pervasiveness keeps alive the symbolism and the faith that make life meaningful.

CHAPTER 4

REGIONALISM

1. The Colonial Tradition

EVERYTHING that we have said reflects the colonial tradition and the results of independence. The colonial tradition was centralist, hierarchical, and authoritarian. The rebellions which forged the independent American nations failed to alter this basic attitude toward government and society, which made centralism, hierarchy, and authoritarianism "natural" and "meritable."

Certainly many things changed in Latin America as a result of independence, but the idea of a government and society which molded and adapted all changes to its own compulsive sense of right and good remained. And where the idea failed, as it did in the case of political identity and fealty, it gave vent not to a new view of the nature of authority, but to countless rebellions which sought to re-establish the grounds of an older fealty.

Until independence everything in America emanated from the Crown. The authoritarian order symbolized by *Yo el Rey*—"I, the King"—sanctioned every law, every act, every office, and every part of the hierarchical structure. Each individual's place, from that of the Negro slave to the *criollo* nobleman and the semi-regal viceroy from Spain, was defined by law and enforced in the name of the king. The criminal condemned to death, the populace that came to watch the execution, and the judge who read the sentence all accepted the proposition that the will of the king was the law of the land. Whatever criticism might be made against the government—that it was foolish, cruel, or stupid, for example—the symbol of authority remained sacred. Moreover, the king had no competitor. It is a matter of great significance that the Mexican Revolution under Father Hidalgo had as its slogan, in the beginning at least: "Down with bad government. Long live the King." When the king disappeared from the scene following independence, the symbol of all authority, not merely political authority, also disappeared. I say "all" because even the Church had its place defined and limited by the royal prerogative of *patronato*.

Not only had the recognized symbol of authority disappeared, but no other all-embracing, unquestioned, and fully accepted authority came to take its place. For centuries men had repeated to themselves as the ultimate sanction: "For God and King." They had conquered, governed, enforced the law, and laid down their lives for the king. The king was "divine" and had something of the immutable quality that attached to absolute verity. Now he was gone. There was no one and no way to fill the vacuum, no all-pervasive symbol of authority, of justice, or of right accepted unquestionably by all the people.

Slogans of "Liberty, Equality, and Fraternity," doctrines of constitutionalism, federalism, centralism, movements labeled "Liberalism," "Conservatism," or the "Justicialism" of Perón, resurgent "communism"—none of these has filled the vacuum. The doctrine of "nationalism" has come closer to universal acceptance than any other symbol of authority. But nationalism in Latin America is of recent emergence and still leaves the choice of an acceptable means for representing the nation subject to debate and dispute.

The failure to substitute a universally accepted symbol of authority was the great failure of the independence movement. Much of what has troubled Latin America since is explicable by the absence of a "moral" authority, for in the Latin American tradition, authority that is not "moral" is intolerable.

This absence of "moral" authority is partially a result of the character of the independence movement. The wars of independence had their origin as a protest against the deposition and imprisonment of the Spanish king and the occupancy of Spain by France. The movement really began as an outpouring of loyalty to the Spanish monarch. If it did not end that way—when Ferdinand VII was returned to his country and crowned amidst the delirium of the Spanish people—this is due to many complicated causes. But one of them is peculiarly Spanish and Latin American: the theory that in the absence of the king, popular sovereignty rests in the local communities.

In the Spanish colonies there existed the institution of the *cabildo*—the local town government which alone allowed native-born whites to serve in administrative posts. The *cabildos* claimed popular sovereignty in the absence of the king, which amounted to a repudiation of the Crown's officials serving in America, and was interpreted by them as a threat to themselves and to the rights of Spain in America. The Americans, however, founded their case on the theory that the colonies belonged to the Crown rather than to Spain. The colonies were one of the many jewels that adorned the Spanish Crown and the people of Spain had no powers in America. In the absence of their common king, the colonies, like the kingdoms of Spain, were equally sovereign and equally competent to govern themselves.

2. Impact of Independence

Whichever way one classifies the causes of the independence movement, the fact is that it turned into a prolonged, confused, and in many ways contradictory movement. In Mexico it began as a popular social movement led by a priest, Father Hidalgo, who was in turn excommunicated, defeated, shot, and hung up for the birds to pick at. The movement ended many years later as a conservative uprising against a liberal Spanish constitution. In Venezuela it came to be a war unto the death; in other places it was a war between a small *criollo* minority and the Spanish authorities. It was not an organized movement with a central revolutionary directorate. It had no Continental Congress. It had no single recognized leader like Washington. It had no agency to provide the movement with funds or to authorize recruitment of an army. Each part of the continent fought the war, which lasted from 1810 to 1824, in its own way. If there was no central direction, no centrally recognized leadership, there was also no formally accepted political doctrine. The monarchists and the democrats each had their spokesmen, and in 1816 at the Congress of Tucumán in Argentina there was even some talk about re-establishing an Inca—if one could be found —on the throne of America. Nor were national boundaries clearly defined. The great leaders in South America were San Martín of Argentina, who crossed the Andes and freed Chile and later attempted to free Peru, and Bolívar, who marched with his armies from Venezuela to Bolivia. In the final battle fought on the small plain near Ayancucho at 12,000 feet altitude, the soldiers on the field came from Venezuela, Colombia, Ecuador, Peru, Argentina, and Chile, and among the officers there were Frenchmen and Englishmen who had opposed each other in the Napoleonic Wars. It was a continental, if not an international, army. The war stopped but did not officially end. There was no treaty of peace. There was no recognition of the new states. There was no definite agreement as to the form of government or even as to national boundaries— as, for instance, whether what is now Bolivia was to be a separate nation or whether Central America was a part of Mexico.

Just as there was no Continental Congress, there was no Constitutional Convention where all of the former colonies united to establish a government. In Latin America each separate area went its own way. Central America broke away from Mexico and then splintered into five separate nations. Uruguay, Paraguay, and Bolivia separated themselves from Argentina, Chile from Peru, and Bolívar's attempt to federate the state of *Gran Colombia* (Venezuela, Colombia, and Ecuador) with Peru and Bolivia under a centralized government broke down. Bolívar, who by his energy and leadership had kept the independence movement alive and carried it to success, had to flee for his life. He died on his way into exile at the age of 47, saying that "America is ungovernable. Those who served the revolution plowed the sea."

The tragedy of Bolívar's life was typical of what happened to other great leaders of the independence. San Martín went into exile in Europe, where he wandered around in poverty and neglect until he died a very old man. Antonio José de Sucre, the greatest of Bolívar's generals, was ambushed and murdered while returning home after his many years of disinterested service in war and as administrator in all of the countries freed by the armies of Bolívar. Bernardo O'Higgins, the Chilean hero of independence, was exiled in Peru; Hidalgo and Morelos, the Mexican leaders, had both been killed by the Spaniards, and Iturbide, the soldier who freed Mexico by betraying his supporters and having himself crowned Emperor Iturbide the First, faced a firing squad a few years later. With the great leaders gone, in exile or in the grave, the question of what government was to be or who had a right to govern remained unsettled.

3. The Continuing Hierarchy

During the colonial period the Spanish government and Church officials were at the top of the hierarchy. These were followed by the peninsular merchant, landowner, or mine operator. Later, the *criollo* born of Spanish parents—usually a landowner and sometimes having a claim on a title of nobility acquired by his ancestors in the conquest or inherited from the older nobility or purchased from the Crown—came to the fore. The *criollo* had few political or administrative opportunities. He was, however, a member of the *cabildo* either by himself or through his family. This was the aristocracy.

The life of this aristocracy was a round of official courtesies, each guarding his special prerogatives as a kind of sacred rule of diplomatic protocol, which if once violated ceased to have any value at all. Protocol was the law of life itself. Petty disputes over the interpretation of the rules might go on for years and ultimately be carried to the king in Spain for a final verdict.

Beneath these ruling groups were the Indians, the Negro slaves, the mulattoes and the mestizos, and between them all those classed as *castas*, of which there were twenty different types recognized in Mexico. The Indian and the Negro had their special place defined by the law and custom, as did many of the *castas*.

Independence made a few changes in the hierarchy. The Spanish bureaucrat, whether viceroy or tax collector, was gone, and for a period Spaniards in business in Latin America were mistreated and sometimes expelled; their goods were often expropriated. The *criollo* moved into the first rank, and some mestizos who had been soldiers or petty officers or otherwise enterprising increased their status. The Negro gained a good deal in the independence wars. Like the mestizo, he was often forcibly enlisted in the armies of liberation and then given his freedom. He therefore gained a step. But slavery continued for some time in the different countries—until 1851 in Peru, for instance. The Indian definitely lost by the wars of independence, although in many, perhaps most, of the countries he was in the majority. Certainly this was true in Peru, Bolivia, Ecuador, Central America (except Costa Rica), and Mexico. The Indian lost the benefits of the colonial legislation which had protected him against the white men. The king in Spain could be impartial between the Indian and the *criollo* or mestizo, but the new officials who stood to benefit at the expense of the Indian were less likely to enforce the law equitably between them. And there were, in Bolivia for instance, cases of sheer rapacity on the part of the government against Indian communities, who were driven from their lands, which were then given to the members of the government who had instigated the action.

The *criollo* upper class, small, proud, and wealthy, who had made the revolution against Spain, now assumed all available political power, but had no mandate except the revolution and no support from the populace. There was no populace; the Indian, the Negro, the mestizo, and the mulatto were the mass of the people, and they had no political awareness or participation. Economically, socially, and politically, power had fallen into the hands of a small oligarchy, which found effective government impossible because it could not control the military who, during fourteen years of revolution, had learned to live off the land, the landlord, the merchant, and the priest. The wars of independence were financed by forced exactions—sometimes a town was ordered to provide a certain amount within 24 hours or have its wealthiest citizens face a firing squad. True, the citizens were probably Spaniards, but the habit outlived the wars of independence. The army had acquired the art of living off the country and exacting from the government all there was to be had. The *criollo* oligarchy found it difficult to agree among themselves or with the new army generals who, as time went by, were increasingly recruited from the mestizos. The army generals made it hard for the government to govern and difficult for it to stay in office. Over a period of many years a government come to power could rarely survive as long as twelve months. It went out of office as it came in—by revolution.

4. Regionalism

The failure of the central government to govern merely strengthened what was natural to the terrain and the tradition—regionalism. Local leadership, the local *caudillo*, was a natural continuum of the independence movement and gained from the loss of prestige and power by the central government. From the very early days of the wars of independence in Argentina, Peru, Bolivia, Mexico, Venezuela, and most other places, regionalism became the dominant note in the social, economic, and political life of the area. Any government at the center had to find a way to get along with the region, and that meant the regional *caudillo*. The *caudillo* continued at the local level the kind of government traditionally expected from the center; it was both absolute and authoritarian and rested on the same hierarchical social structure that had always prevailed. Only the Spaniards were gone.

The Spanish colonial government had to an extent prepared Latin America for this emergence of the regional *caudillo* by excluding native-born American whites from administration, except in the *cabildo*. What communication the various localities had had in the past with the outside had long been confined to channels that led to the king in Spain. Now, with the passing of the king and all of his servants in America, the only organ of government that remained was, therefore, the local, regional, and isolated *cabildo*. The *cabildo* was staffed by local *hacendados* who elected and re-elected each other to office annually. Martín José Artigas, for instance, father of the great national hero of Uruguay, was ten times a member of the *cabildo* of Montevideo.

The only real wealth or prestige in most places was in land, and as one moved from the capital to the smaller cities and village centers, the landed aristocracy dominated both the countryside and the town and all local authority was in its hands. The local *caudillo* was also a large local landowner. A good example of this is the Terrazas family in Chihuahua in Mexico, or the Rosas and Urquiza families in Argentina.

Except in Chile, from 50 to 100 years passed before the local region could be sufficiently subordinated to the center to make national government more than an aspiration. In Argentina, after a series of civil wars, it was not until 1880 that a national government could be established with the consent of all the provinces. Mexico is a good example of continuing disturbance. It did not find national unity until the Díaz dictatorship imposed it, and one could argue that Mexico did not become a nation in which the regions were truly subordinate until after the

Revolution of 1910 had destroyed the hacienda system and weakened the hierarchical structure.

In effect, the enforcement of the law and the protection of life fell into the hands of the hacienda. As Ponciano Arriaga enumerated the functions of the hacienda, it embraced all of government. In its lordly lands it sanctioned and executed the law, administered justice, exercised the civil power, exacted contributions and imposed fines, kept its own jails and stocks, punished the recalcitrant, monopolized commerce, and prohibited the exercise of any industry other than that on the plantation. The functionaries who exercised the powers of civil officials were employees or tenants of the plantation and dependents of its owners and they were incapable of performing their duties except as agents subject to the will of their employer. The rules enforced were not mere matters of civil law but included the regulations of the hacienda concerning wages, methods of payment, the use of local currency (that circulated only on the plantation), the enforcement of the rules of peonage preventing individuals who had a debt to the hacienda from leaving, and suppression of all commerce except in the *tienda de Raya* (hacienda store). The violence that followed independence made every hacienda a kind of isolated political and juridical province and all that has followed in Latin American politics stems from this primordial fact. What had once been a centralized imperial administration broke into semi-independent "feudal" provinces with "lands sufficient to form a kingdom," as graphically phrased by Count Revilla Gigedo, a former viceroy of Mexico.

CHAPTER 5

THE HACIENDA

1. The Structure of the Hacienda

THE HACIENDA played a special role in Latin America. It would be no exaggeration to say that the hacienda—or the fazenda, as it is known in Brazil—set the tone and determined the quality of Latin American culture during the nineteenth century and until the First World War. In some instances—in Ecuador, Chile, Peru, in Argentina, and other areas as well—its influence has continued up to the present. This is not an argument for unitary causation. Other factors, such as the Spanish tradition, the presence of the Indian and the Negro, the broad influence of the Church, and the impact of the larger world, deserve consideration. But here we are dealing with those areas where over one half of the population is rural and where the typical agricultural holding is large. The U.N. estimated in 1951 that plots of over 15,000 acres, though comprising only 1½ per cent of all private holdings, accounted for half of all the land in agriculture in Latin America. Some of these holdings are very extensive indeed. There once were plantations in Mexico of 1,000,000 acres and similar units still exist in Brazil and in other countries.

A few examples will make this clear. In Mexico as late as 1923, 114 owners held 25 per cent of the land. In 1958 in Argentina, 283 families owned 17 per cent of the province of Buenos Aires. In Uruguay, 787 proprietors controlled 30 per cent of the land in use. In Colombia, less than 1 per cent of the owners held 42.2 per cent of all land in use, while in Cuba in 1955, 1.5 per cent had title to 46 per cent of the acreage under cultivation.

Before entering into a discussion of the hacienda as such, it is useful to note that at least in the Andean countries, Central America, and Mexico there were two distinctive agricultural systems—the hacienda and the village community. In Guatemala, for instance, the hacienda occupied the valley, the slopes, and the rolling hills—the best agricultural lands. The Indian villages, on the other hand, were limited to the steep mountains, the inaccessible areas, and the poor soil. This was also true in Mexico and Bolivia; it is true today in Ecuador and Peru. The hacienda has the best agricultural lands, and the Indian or mestizo villages the poorest. The village may be communal, following an older Indian tradition, or it may have adopted every possible variation that lies between collective and individual ownership.

But the village is a community with its own local traditional government where the entire male population participates in the governmental process. It looks after its own public works, its policing, and its roads; it builds a common school if there is to be one and cares for the church. Each individual as he grows up takes his turn in carrying out the various tasks that the community requires. In the case of Amatanango in Chiapas in Mexico, for example, each boy begins as a messenger for the town government, in time he becomes one of the village policemen, and after satisfying all of the required offices in the civil government and in the Church, ends up as an *anciano*, one of the elders on the council governing the community. Each Indian or mestizo village has its own collective personality. Each member has a recognized place of his own and a defined relationship to all the others. He is a participant in government and Church because he has regular functions to perform in both.

This village may be next to a hacienda—and there are cases where a village has somehow survived, although surrounded by a hacienda—but generally speaking, the rural world divides sharply between the hacienda in the valley and the village on the steep mountainsides. Between these two agricultural organizations there has always been friction, the hacienda encroaching upon the village, absorbing its woods, pastures, and water supply, and the village every now and then rising in rebellion, protesting, or going to court. The story is an old one and goes back to the early days after the conquest when the Indians crowded the offices of the Spanish officials, asking for protection against the *hacendado* who was encroaching upon their lands.

After independence, the Indians were less able to find support against the neighboring hacienda. The history of rural land holdings after independence is one in which—

in the name of liberalism, equality, and individual rights
—the Indian was increasingly dispossessed of his lands in
favor of the hacienda. Property taken from the Church by
the new national governments tended to swell the size of
the haciendas and the power and prestige of the *hacendados*. The little villages during the same period decreased
in number, size, and significance. The relatively few and
isolated areas where they increased in number, as in southern Chile, southern Brazil, and some places in Argentina,
had little bearing on the general trend. The private hacienda carried everything before it.

The hacienda is not just an agricultural property owned
by an individual. The hacienda is a society, under private
auspices. It is an entire social system and governs the life
of those attached to it from the cradle to the grave. It en-
compasses economics, politics, education, social activities,
and industrial development. A curious phenomenon in
Latin American intellectual life is that the hacienda,
which is so all-embracing in its influence is, except in an
occasional novel, never written about or seriously studied.
It is, or was, so much part of the environment that the intellectuals, who were mostly children of the hacienda,
were no more conscious of its existence than we are of the
air we breathe. When the Latin American sociologist
looked for something to write about, he worried about the
unemployed in London, or about the new sugar and banana plantations in foreign lands. But the hacienda, which
had a determining effect on the country's culture, was
something he was hardly aware of.

The hacienda as a society may be described by saying
that it was—and is—an economic and social system that
seeks to achieve self-sufficiency and autarchy on a local

scale. It seeks this not as a matter of malice, but as a matter of logic. Each unit expands until it has within its own borders all that it needs—salt from the sea, *panela* (black, unrefined sugar) from its own cane fields, corn, barley, wheat, coconuts, bananas, apples, and pears. All of this depends upon where the hacienda is located. If it can run from the seacoast to the mountain top, from the river bottom where sugar cane will grow to the snow line, it can raise all of the crops that will grow in all the climates. Not all haciendas—not any perhaps—satisfy this ideal completely, but that is the aim of hacienda organization: to buy nothing; to raise and make everything within the limits of its own boundaries. The big house is built from the timbers found on the land—and these may be, as I have seen them, mahogany. The furniture is made at home. The cloth is woven there from wool shorn off home-grown sheep. The llamas that graze in the hills, the oxen and the horses are raised and broken where they were born. The saddles, bridles, and harnesses are made from the hides of the slaughtered animals. The wooden plow, the wagon, the windmill for the grinding of the corn, or the water mill for the grinding of cane are all fabricated locally. The table may be loaded at a meal with every kind of meat, grain, and fruit, and all of these—the table itself, the house, and the servants as well—will have been raised, contrived, conserved, grown on the place. Even the tablecloth that covers the table, the sandals of the servants if they are not barefooted, and perhaps the Indian musician who sits behind the screen and plays his old songs on his homemade instrument are from the plantation. I know this from personal experience on a plantation in the province of Ayacucho in Peru.

The people on the plantation are born there. They cannot leave because they may be in debt, or because there is no place to go. This is home and every other place is foreign. Here too their fathers and grandfathers were born and are buried. If the place changes hands, they change with it. In 1948 the leading newspaper in La Paz, Bolivia, carried an advertisement offering for sale on the main highway a half hour from the capital of the country a hacienda with 500 acres of land, 50 sheep, much water, and 20 peons. Similar advertisements have appeared in Ecuador and Chile even more recently. The point is that what we are dealing with is a closed system—economically, socially, politically, and culturally.

The hacienda is a way of life rather than a business. It is not an investment. It was inherited. It is operated with the exenditure of as little cash as possible. If the hacienda is large, there may be a couple of hundred or more families residing within its borders. These are scattered in groups of five or ten families in different parts of the hacienda, depending on the kind of crops grown and the terrain. The laborer on the hacienda usually has a hut, which he has built, and a given amount of land, which he works himself or shares.

The hacienda provides the land, the work animals, and the seed, and the peon carries the *hacendado's* share of the crop to the granary near the big house. The hacienda will also receive annually one out of the ten or twelve sheep grazed on hacienda lands by Indians who do not live there. The size of the share is determined by the crop and the tradition of the hacienda. In addition, the Indian also owes the landlord a given number of days of work each week throughout the year. This practice varies. It might be one day's work a week for each hectare of land or so many days a week for living on the land. The families might also owe a certain amount of service in the big house. Thus the hacienda has its labor supplied to it without the use of money. If there are 200 families on the hacienda and if they each owe only one day's work a week for each of two hectares allotted to each family, the hacienda would command 400 workdays each week.

The neighboring villages provide another source of labor. These workers are also not paid in wages. Instead, the Indians are charged so much for the grazing of each animal and are required to pay the debt in labor. This is not an uncommon practice.

This labor is used by the hacienda for working the lands it tills on its own account. These lands might be in sugar cane, from which it can grind sugar, using either oxen or water power in a small homemade *trapiche* (water- or mule-driven factory), squeeze out the juice and make *panela*, and manufacture rum as well. Or its cash crop may be coffee, cocoa, or other products which can be carried to the market on the backs of mules or men, over steep mountains and through narrow gorges to the nearest railroad station or, more recently, to the nearest automobile road or to the nearest town. The cash crop can be raised, harvested, and delivered part or all the way to the nearest market without the expenditure of any cash.

In a curious way, the hacienda is largely beyond the reach of the money economy. Internally it provides, so far as it can, for almost all of its needs. All of the buildings, the draft animals, the tools, the labor supply are derived from internal operations. The seed the hacienda supplies to the sharecroppers comes out of the storehouses in which it was deposited in the fall. If the laborers run short of food or other supplies, these can be purchased in the hacienda store—*tienda de Raya* in Mexican parlance, "company store" in ours.

The peon will pay no cash for his purchases for he has none. His account will be kept in a little book by a storekeeper, usually some distant relative or *compadre* of the *hacendado*. The debt can be liquidated by labor, but it rarely is, and serves to tie the laboring population to the hacienda, since they cannot leave without first paying off their debt. This has long been so. The system began in the colonial era, persisted all through the nineteenth century, and is still found wherever the hacienda survives. It is as hard to kill as were the company store and token coin or script in the mining and lumbering industries in the United States. Token coin has its use on the hacienda for the payment of wages for any extra labor which may be needed beyond that owed by the peons, or for tasks which for some reason lie outside the peon's traditional duties. These token coins, a piece of metal sometimes bearing the name of the hacienda, stamped with *vale un día de trabajo* (it is worth one day's work), can only be exchanged in the hacienda store.

As the hacienda satisfies its own and its community's needs with as little recourse to the market as possible, it buys little and it sells little as well. The distances, the poor roads, the primitive means of communication, make the transport of goods from one part of the country to another difficult and expensive. The hacienda's relatively small income is, so to speak, net profit—taxes on land have always been low and production costs are minimal in monetary terms.

2. The Hacienda as a Society

The hacienda is, however, not merely an economic enterprise. It is also a social, political, and cultural institution. Socially it is a closed community living within its borders. Part of the hacienda population is located near the big house, where the store, the church, the school (if there is one), the repair shops, granaries, the blacksmith, carpenter, and harness shop are also found. The grist mill and the *trapiche* (sugar mill) are also, in all likelihood, near the big house if there is water close by. The stables for the favorite horses, cows, and other animals raised for household use or consumption will be near at hand. The laborers living near the big house tend the livestock and operate the various shops and mills. This is usually the larger part of the hacienda community. The rest are scattered in small groups in different parts of the domain, tending to different functions and raising crops appropriate to the altitude and the climate. Each little ranch hamlet is isolated and far away. It may be anywhere from one to ten miles from the next hamlet, depending on the size of the hacienda. Contacts with the outside world are few indeed, and paths on the hacienda lead mainly to the center where the big house is located. Only one rarely used path leads to another hacienda, and to still another, until the neighboring town is reached, which may be 10, 20, 30, or more miles away.

Community activity takes place in front of the big house

on Sundays when the peons come to church even if there is no priest in regular attendance. All burials, christenings, and marriages, when they are solemnized, are social matters involving the Church and as large a part of the hacienda community as is aware of the occasion. The important feast days are likely to be the Saint's day of the owner or of some favorite member of the family. Then the entire community will turn the event into a holiday with decorations, music, dancing, and drinking. A similar day is given to celebrating the patron saint of the local church. There may be others, depending on the local Indian, mestizo, or Negro traditions. Beyond these festive occasions the hacienda community has no public functions or responsibilities. It is not a governmental unit, an organized parish, or a co-operative. If any vestige of the older Indian community survives on the hacienda, it is unrecognized by the *hacendado*, and what functions it retains must of necessity lie outside of the hacienda.

3. The Hacienda and Politics

There may be, and often is, a bond between the peons on the place and the *hacendado* which goes beyond the formal manager-laborer relation. The *hacendado* may have stood as godfather to many of the children born on the place. He may have a role not as employer primarily but as the head of a family of which all the laborers consider themselves members. The hacienda laborers' community may have an integrity deriving from many years of co-operation, interdependence, and mutual aid. The hacienda is an old institution. It has usually belonged to the same family over many generations, sometimes for centuries. Isolation from the larger world, time, circumstance, and the need for mutual protection have tended to bring the haciendas within the same region close to each other. By intermarriage the owner of the hacienda is likely to be related to most of the proprietors of the neighboring properties, so that the *hacendados* of a particular region comprise a large family extended over a vast area where everyone knows and is related to everyone else.

In time, one or another of these closely knit families will have acquired an ascendancy over the others and assumed a kind of traditional leadership over the region. Given the loyalty of family members to each other and the godfather relation that always exists, you have the basis for political power and regional *caciquismo*. Because of the turbulence and instability that followed independence, *caciquismo* served the important end of protecting its own. The interdependence of the regional hacienda owners became a pattern for self-protection and defense —either military or political. The rule that developed, and was logically required by the situation, was that each region followed its own leader—if necessary, against the national one. The local leaders each had a following which belonged only to them, and the national leader depended upon their support.

In that situation the power of the national leader tended to be unstable, temporary, and subject to many hazards. He really lived on borrowed strength. The power of the local *cacique* was very great and beyond the effective control of the central government. The hacienda thus supported a system of local *caciquismo*, which became a major cause of political instability. The hacienda community's fealty gave the *hacendado* a power which was immediate and direct, and a group of related and interdependent *hacendados* were able to control an entire region.

The hacienda also dominated the small neighboring city and prevented it from developing economically or politically. The complaint so often heard in the Latin American smaller town, that it has no "movement," that it is "dead," is true and no great mystery. The haciendas which surround the town buy little. Their peons have no money and the hacienda grows and manufactures very nearly all that it requires. The town has no important distributing function. The hacienda sells relatively little, considering its size and the number of people living on it. What it does sell is marketed, usually, on a wholesale basis by some agent employed by the hacienda, or by a member of the family, and is sent on, if possible to a larger city at a distance, with the result that the smaller neighboring city is bypassed. Even the mule pack carrying the hacienda goods to the city or the nearest railroad belongs to the hacienda.

The better houses in the town usually belong to the neighboring haciendas and are occupied by some members of the family, probably an old mother, or a brother who does not like to live on the hacienda or who has some professional interest. The children of the *hacendado* also are in this house during the school year. The servants in the house come from the hacienda and are a permanent part of the household, requiring no money wage. In the mountains of Peru the house has the service of one or more *pongos* (unpaid servants) who each work in the house for a week, then go back to the hacienda. This is part of their payment for the few hectares of land they till on the hacienda. In addition, the house is supplied from the hacienda with a large part of its needs—wheat, barley, rice, corn, whatever fruits are raised, and, depending on the distance, butter, cheese, and whatever else the climate will allow to be transported. As a result, the big houses in the town are not important participants in the local market.

All of this and much more has kept the town commercially inactive. If the hacienda dominates the town economically, it does so politically as well. The great family will control every local office, from the colonel of the local militia to the rural police. The tax gatherer, the mayor, the judge, the postmaster, will be related directly or through marriage or as godfathers to members of the family. And unless the president of the country feels strong enough to be indifferent to the interest and pride of the local leadership, he will not impose "foreigners" on the locality.

4. The Future of the Hacienda

If we summarize the role of the hacienda in the development of Latin America we will see that it has been—and continues to be, where haciendas still exist—an isolating and conservative influence. Its traditional sharecropping system prevented the use of improved machinery, methods, or seeds. It tied its labor force to the property and kept mobility to a minimum. It was a dampening influence on commercial development because it bought and sold relatively little in the open market. Its huge expanse, linked only by paths leading to the big house, discouraged road building. It established and maintained a system of dependence between the *hacendado* and his peons which perpetuated an authoritarian tradition of master and very humble servant (I saw in Bolivia the Indians on a plantation bend their knees and kiss the hands of the *hacendado*). It prevented the accumulation of capital, required no investment, called for no change, did nothing to prevent soil erosion and improve agricultural techniques. The hacienda family controlled the local political scene and set the tone socially. It paid little taxes and neglected, or was unable, to put all of its resources to good use.

Perhaps most serious of all is that the hacienda fostered and maintained the *hacendado* as a social ideal—a superior being possessed of broad acres and numerous servants, dominant, domineering, patronizing, and paternal, with no restrictions between himself and the peon on the plantation. All other elements in society—craftsmen, businessmen, entrepreneurs, and the entire middle class —were looked upon with disdain as a necessary affliction that had at best to be suffered. The *hacendado* was the master of all he surveyed and the world looked good to him. It gave him economic stability, social prestige, political power, affluence, and leisure. Those of his children who did not remain on the hacienda went off to the capital of the country, attended the university, and became lawyers, doctors, or literary men. Many of them combined literature with a profession. They might also meddle in politics, especially if the administration was one which their family—the extended family, the people who came from the same region, who followed the same local traditional leadership—had helped to bring into office.

Education fitted the ideal. Primary schooling for the

mass of the people was a matter of indifference; higher education in the main led to a limited number of professions—medicine, law, and to a much lesser degree civil engineering. In earlier days, the university also taught theology. The emphasis more recently has been on philosophy and literature. Thus if Latin America has fallen behind the United States and Western Europe in industrial expansion, in the development of politically stable and democratic government, and in the growth of an educational system adequate for modern needs, much of the fault lies with the hacienda system.

It has in fact reached in impasse from which it cannot escape. The pressure for economic, political, and social change is building so rapidly that the hacienda system cannot escape the challenge, and it cannot meet it. *The hacienda has no built-in device that will allow for reform of the system,* that will enable it to transform itself so as to survive and adjust to the present. It has found no way of meeting the challenges of television and atomic energy— and, if you like, of psychoanalysis and Karl Marx—and yet it cannot remain indifferent to them.

In the two countries where the hacienda has been repudiated, Mexico and Bolivia, it was done by revolution. Revolution, too, has transferred to the government the traditional commercial plantation in Cuba. The question of whether there is another way of dealing with impending change remains to be seen. I say "impending," for it would require undue self-confidence to assume that the demands for industrialism and democracy can be met without seriously affecting the total role of the hacienda. What is happening in a small way in Peru perhaps suggests that governments can, if they have the energy, vision, and political courage, attempt a program of agrarian reform that meets the modern challenge without requiring a social convulsion. But who can say that the organized forces of government would be able to move fast enough to satisfy the increasing social and economic pressure which such policies would stimulate? I am not suggesting that cataclysm is inevitable. But what is inevitable if Latin America is to industrialize effectively, and meet the demands for a higher standard of living and a more democratic society, is a wide agrarian reform which is not compatible with the survival of the hacienda system.

There are other ways than revolution of dealing with the hacienda system, but they have not been tried, and there is no way of knowing how effective they might prove. In Ecuador, for instance, it is estimated that one half of the haciendas belong to the government, held by *beneficencia* (public charity). These lands have been in the hands of the government since 1908, when they were taken from the Church. They are rented to *hacendados* and worked on the old system. It has been suggested that the government could begin dividing these haciendas among the Indians and thus significantly change the conditions of the peasant without raising issues of legality or revolution. In the neighborhood of Loja in southern Ecuador, the descendants of the original colonial *hacendados* have found the operation of the hacienda unsatisfactory as a way of life, and the Indians, by forming themselves into co-operatives, have, by paying small amounts over a period of years, gradually repurchased the land which was theirs at the time of the conquest.

It has also been suggested that the governments develop a systematic program for buying haciendas that come on the market and breaking them up into small holdings, which peasants can then purchase with whatever aid and credit can be made available. A study of the agrarian problem is currently being made by the United Nations Food and Agriculture Organization, apparently at the request of some of the governments concerned with the issues involved. Whether these and other possible programs can be implemented with the financial resources available to governments without changing their present political and social orientation remains to be seen. But the matter is urgent. There is no reason to assume that Mexico, Bolivia, and Cuba will forever remain isolated examples of agrarian change.

This discussion does not include the issues raised by the large commercial plantation in sugar, bananas, and other crops grown for the international market. The fact that these large plantations may be foreign-owned is only a minor complication to a difficult problem. Any attempt to apply agrarian reform policies to these commercial plantations must take into account the fact that they are efficiently operated, require a high degree of scientific and technical skill, have a foreign market which they control or have to meet the world price at which the commodity is selling, and yield a cash income per acre higher than any other crop that could be grown. These are questions of such magnitude, especially where the government gets a large part of its income from the export of a single commodity, that any government policy that would price the commodity out of the market, reduce the required investment, or cut down efficiency would not necessarily improve the economic well-being of either the peasantry or the government. The fact that the properties have to be paid for merely increases the difficulties. But it must be clear that in their modern form these enterprises are relatively new, are to a considerable extent foreign-owned and foreign-managed, and are so large that they tend to dwarf all other domestic enterprise.

This raises political questions that may in fact be insoluble—a hard thing to recognize and to accept. But politically a certain institution may prove to be intolerable even if it can be shown to be highly beneficial economically. The large modern plantation is probably more like a factory than a farm, and if it were possible for modern management, the workers, and the government to believe that they are involved in an industrial rather than an agricultural enterprise, then issues other than land reform would control whatever controversies might arise.

Modern sugar and banana plantations are, however, not the major issue in any discussion of the hacienda. These enterprises, except in isolated areas like Cuba, are only a small part of the total agricultural plant. The hacienda is another matter. It has set the tone for a whole society and —while it differs greatly between Argentina and Peru, for instance—it has been a major factor in shaping the cultural development of the area and the educational system as well.

CHAPTER 6

EDUCATION

1. The School Record

IN THE KIND of world we have been describing, education takes on special forms. The relatively small group of Europeans and their descendants have had an education fitting the aristocratic, authoritarian role that tradition has demanded of them. It has given them refinements and interests seemingly natural to "superior" persons in an authoritarian society, while education for the mass of the people at public expense has been limited and of poor quality. This whole matter is a delicate and sensitive issue, hard to deal with and hard to evaluate.

We must always begin by remembering that the universities in Lima and Mexico are each a century older than Harvard, and that in Mexico, within a few years after the conquest, the Franciscans carried on a most notable educational enterprise where, among other things, Indian boys learned to read Latin and some became good Latinists. The Order of Jesus also made significant contributions in the field of education among *criollos* and Indians.

But all of this is in the background. The published figures, whatever their accuracy, record that in mid-nineteenth century at least one half of the people in Latin America could neither read nor write. That would mean something like 70,000,000 to 80,000,000 people. Today, countries like Argentina, Chile, Uruguay, and Costa Rica can boast of a literacy rate of 80 per cent or more, while in Bolivia, El Salvador, and Guatemala the people counted as literate number somewhere around 30 in each 100. In Haiti, only about 10 per cent can read and write. These figures are probably somewhat optimistic. It has been estimated that something like four to five years of primary schooling are required before it can be assumed that the child will not fall back into illiteracy. If this is the case, then there are many more people who are functionally illiterate than is indicated by the published figures.

On the whole, the children who enter primary school do not finish. This is especially true in rural districts. In rural Brazil, of the 12,700,000 children between the ages of seven and fourteen, over 5,000,000 are not in school, and of those who are, more than half abandon their studies in the first year. According to a U.N. study, less than 1 per cent of those entering rural schools reach the fifth grade, whereas in urban schools the figure is at least 9 per cent. In 14 Latin American countries, only 1.7 per cent of children of school age reach the highest primary grade. In Mexico, where there is great interest in education, out of 20,000 rural schools, over 16,000 have only three grades.

In Guatemala only 5.2 per cent of rural schoolchildren reach the third grade. In contrast, in the United States, 22.2 per cent of the entire population is enrolled in schools. For Brazil the figure is 8.9 per cent, in Guatemala 7 per cent, in Colombia 10 per cent, and in Haiti 1.7 per cent. The record of Argentina, Chile, Uruguay, and Costa Rica is very much better, and it ought to be repeated that the urban school situation is always better than the rural. But taken as a whole, for an area dedicated to democratic government and aiming at industrialization, the educational program leaves much to be desired. The difficulties are many and not easy to overcome.

As we have already seen, Latin America's population is growing very fast. This means that the proportion of children in the total population is relatively large. The children of school age—five to 14—are proportionately twice as numerous in the Latin American countries as they are in Western Europe. In the more industrialized countries of Europe, there are four adults to every child of school age, while there are only two in Latin America. The relative burden—all other things being equal—of the educational costs to be borne by each individual would therefore be twice as great in Latin America as it would be in England or Belgium. And, in addition, this burden falls on people who have a much lower income to begin with, living in countries where industrial investment per capita is lower and in an area where productivity per individual is smaller. This, however, is only part of the difficulty.

In many of the countries in Latin America there is the additional impediment of languages other than Spanish spoken by a considerable part—in some cases, by a majority—of the population. Where does the enthusiast for popular education find teachers who know the native language? How does he prepare the schoolroom materials so as to make them meaningful? How does he persuade the parents to send their children to school? How does he interpret to the little children of an entirely different cultural universe the values derived from European antecedents? These problems might well task the ingenuity and the determination of even the most idealistic reformer. I always recall the little Chamula child of about seven or eight who had learned Spanish in the town where his mother had been working, and who now acted as an interpreter for his teacher to some dozen other Chamula children of about his own age. It was heroic and pathetic at the same time. Only the greatest devotion would explain the effort to pass on European culture and the ideals of Mexican nationalism through the medium of this little child. But he was the only interpreter available for the task at hand. It was pathetic, for the one or two years' schooling that was to be had in that small schoolroom would mean very little to those children by the time they came to be grown men.

At least half of the people in Bolivia, Ecuador, Guatemala, and Peru cannot understand Spanish. Even in families where the father speaks it, Indian children do not learn it. At home the mother tongue is Quiche, Aymara, Trique, or whatever the language of the Indian group happens to be. The language barrier is more formidable than enthusiasts who would like to convert Indians into good nationals like to believe.

I am reminded of Viceroy Francisco de Toledo, who in 1572 wrote to the king of Spain that, on visiting Lake Titacaca, he had found it was impossible to preach the Christian gospel in Aymara, for it was a barbarous language.

He had, therefore, given orders that within six months all the Aymara people were to learn Quechua, for that was a sweet and easy manner of speech and good for the preaching of the gospel. In 1940 I gave a talk to a group of Indians in a school for Indian children in that same area. It had to be translated from Spanish into Quechua and then by a Quechua Indian into Aymara. Conceivably, modern methods are more efficient than those of Viceroy Francisco de Toledo, but they are not easy and it will take time—perhaps more time than patience will allow for.

Of course, other factors besides the school contribute to the spreading of the Spanish language. The road, the automobile, the town, all help to weaken the linguistic barrier between Indian and mestizo. But if education also teaches the Indian nationalism—nationalism based upon language and race—and if the Quechua and Aymara learn to love their language as the Irish learned to love their Gaelic, then literacy may have consequences other than those foreseen by the men and women who are devoting their energies to teaching the people to read and write.

2. Education and Culture

This raises another question: how effective is a literacy campaign in a country where there are no books for the mass of the people, no magazines, no newspapers, in fact, no reading matter? A few examples will make the point. Circulation of daily newspapers in Venezuela in 1947 equaled 6 per cent of population; in Guatemala, 1.6 per cent; Honduras, 1.5 per cent; Nicaragua, 2.3 per cent; and Colombia, 4.9 per cent.

The literacy campaigns, and there have been a number, have accomplished but little. For literacy is not something by itself. It is an expression of a total cultural situation. Where reading and writing is not used because no one writes letters, newspapers are unknown, and there is nothing to read—because even if one did once go to school, one's first-grade primer has disappeared, moldered away with time—it is easy to forget the alphabet one may have acquired in the primary grade.

It is hard for city dwellers here or in Latin America to visualize the poverty of literary materials in the ordinary rural school and rural community. Since everything in the school usually comes from the central ministry of education, the schoolteacher will receive a scant supply of schoolroom writing material, a blackboard and chalk, first- and second-grade primers, and sometimes not even these limited items.

I remember in the thirties traveling through Oaxaca, in Mexico, with the director of rural education of the state, and one of the things he presented to the schools in the mountains was a piece of black cloth, cut from a roll, that could be used as a blackboard, along with some pieces of chalk. This was always accepted with great appreciation by the elders of the community, for until then the school had lacked even these simple aids to instruction.

In some places the teacher may receive a magazine published by the ministry of education and filled with articles on the theory of education, which he will probably not understand. In most rural schools even the teacher may have scant book learning. In Haiti more than half of the teachers have had no formal preparation for their job, while in Brazil half of the teachers in primary schools have only had a primary education.

Suddenly to provide schooling adequate to the needs of a modern nation is a Herculean task. In a country like the United States the schools grew as the population increased. Each separate community in its own way contrived to find the means to have a school and a teacher, and did it on its own initiative without waiting on or expecting aid from the government. The way it was done varied with the county and township and was locally financed. In Latin America the case is very different. The schools are usually maintained, supported, and supervised by the national government. The national government appoints the teachers, builds or rents the schools, plans the program, supplies the classroom materials, and orders, regulates, and examines everything, from the school desk and the blackboard to the final examination and the morals of the teacher.

In the capital, an educational bureaucracy—well intentioned, perhaps well trained, knowing exactly what is to be done and how to do it—gives orders in long *reglamentos* to teachers off in the jungle or in some mountain crevice and fills the air with sounds of activity though with little meaning for those far distant from the capital. In periods of political instability—and political instability has been something of a norm in the last quarter of a century —the educational directors at the center change with each government, the old plans are thrown out, new plans devised because they are said to be better, and before these new plans can really take effect, a change in government will bring a new minister of education, who will have a newer and better plan that will also fail of fulfillment.

These are pessimistic views—but how can one run away from the facts? The unstable political situation has seriously impeded the growth of an adequate school system and will continue to do so. Centralization makes every school in the nation (not all nations have the same degree of centralization) dependent upon the ministry of education, but the minister of education is an appointee of the president and changes with the president.

This point is worth keeping in mind in contemplating the task that lies ahead of any government that would really meet the educational needs of a modern nation. The central government must find, build, rent, or appropriate schools for the 50 or more per cent of the school population now without schools. It must find, educate, and draft double the number of teachers it now has and place them on the national payroll. It must print twice as many books and notebooks, procure twice as many pencils and blackboards. It must double the number of school inspectors, bookkeepers, clerks, supervisors, and normal schools for the training of teachers. It must do all of this and a great deal more, and it must do it in a hurry. The population is growing so fast that at the moment the school system is losing ground. The means must be found to double the education budget, although in some countries it is already large. When the president has done all of this—and no one else can do it—he will have universalized the present situation: a little over 1 per cent of all the children of school age will complete the fifth or sixth grade and half of the children matriculating will not go beyond the first year. The amount of literacy will have increased but slightly, while the extent of functional illiteracy will probably have doubled.

Centralization demands that the national government do it all, and the central government expects to do it all, or leave it undone. But what is required within the national ideal is a rural and urban school system that will give at least a primary-grade education of six to eight years for all the children everywhere, and do it soon—and this the government cannot do. Physical impediments of geography, different languages, poverty, insufficient teachers, schools, and money make the demand for a universal primary education for all children an ideal that can, at present, have no fulfillment.

To make the project possible and reasonable, the country would have to be suddenly endowed with an industrial system, an economy, a social structure, and a national income sufficiently large and sufficiently well distributed so as to make it inevitable that all the parents of all the children would insist that each child receive the training he needs to enable him to find a place in this new society. Such a project would also require the quite sudden appearance of adequately trained teachers in sufficient numbers, as well as administrators willing and able to organize and manage so large an undertaking. These things are not done by sheer exercise of will. They have to grow together. Those who are concerned with education would do well to recognize that the educational system is a function of the total society and cannot be treated in isolation. One could say that a society has an educational establishment appropriate to its culture. The school system changes as the society changes, and there are no miracles to be looked for.

3. The Mexican Experience

In this connection it is interesting to have a look at the quite remarkable Mexican experience in rural education.

The Mexican educational effort came out of the revolution and had in its initial days the aim of remaking the nation and bringing the rural folk, including the Indian, into closer contact with the modern world. Beginning in 1923 under the leadership of José Vasconcelos, and later of Moisés Sáenz and Rafael Ramirez, an attempt was made to carry the school to even the most isolated villages. Starting with inadequate funds, insufficient teachers, and a not too clear idea of what could be done, the movement had the advantage of enthusiasm and faith in the powers of the revolution to redeem the rural population from the effects of peonage and to incorporate the Indian into the new nation. Toward these goals, the school was expected to make a major contribution.

The important lesson for the future revealed by this undertaking was that the rural community, no matter how poor and abandoned, could become an active participant in a system of rural education. Having neither money nor trained personnel, the Ministry of Education resorted to sending "missionaries" on horseback to the villages in the mountains to preach the gospel of learning for the children. The villagers were gathered together and the difficulties and prospects were discussed in a kind of open assembly. It soon became apparent that the communities would build the school themselves. The missionary turned architect, and the men, women, and children in their spare time and on Sundays and holidays gathered and hewed stones, mixed lime, worked the adobe, and built the school on land the community had given for the purpose. In a short time over 6,000 rural schools were built by the villages without any cost to the central government, and having built them, the villagers felt as if the schools belonged to them.

The missionaries and officials in the ministry—without experience and with no confining traditions except the ideal of using the school as an agency of social improvement—permitted themselves to be influenced by the communities who wanted the school to be useful to the village. Out of this there developed, without any initial plan, a body of what came to be called *anexos* to the school. The basketball field would be one *anexo*. A lamp for the school, so that it could be used by the adults in the evenings, would be another such *anexo*. A shower bath made out of a tin can raised on poles into which one child poured water while another stood beneath it and got himself washed was another. These examples suggest the many possibilities that lay hidden in this kind of attitude toward the rural school.

It soon turned out that the *anexos* were the important part of the rural school. They included such things as a school garden, a house for the teacher, and a plot of land given to the school and worked by the adults for the purpose of providing additional income for the school or for the schoolteacher. The school also developed a kitchen where the women could learn to cook. It had a sewing machine, a barber shop where older boys cut the hair of the younger ones, and a medical kit or primitive dispensary where the teacher acted as nurse and applied iodine, bandages, and had some other simple remedies. There was no standardization in these matters. Each school acquired those *anexos* most convenient to its particular community.

The rural school came to be judged primarily not by its

reading and writing but by its *anexos*—one school boasted of 33 separate activities in addition to teaching the three R's. One result was that the school was always open and members of the community participated in its goings-on. Another consequence was the formation of "committees" of villagers to look after the various *anexos:* school sanitation, the school garden, the school plot, the school furniture, attendance, the night school, and so forth. The school was a busy place indeed. One teacher remarked that the school never closed. "When I get tired I take a rest."

These many activities gradually grew into a kind of theory. The rural school was meant to be the agency for teaching the people to make the best use of their immediate environment and their immediate resources. It was implicitly recognized that beyond its immediate resources the rural village had nothing really dependable that it could fall back upon. How to learn to live the good life here in this village, and how to bring to the villagers applicable skills and knowledge available in the outside world at a cost that they could afford became the essentials of educational doctrine. This was in the nature of a philosophy of education for the rural population. It was a new view of the proper role of a rural school. This kind of activity in the rural schools tended to bring the school and the community close together. As has been suggested, the most important lesson that this movement taught was that there is a latent initiative and enthusiasm in the community that, once awakened, can be of great help in the development of rural education.

In 1960, thirty-seven years after this movement got underway, Mexico had some 20,000 rural schools, and the government prides itself on its large educational budget.

But the vast majority of rural schools do not go beyond the third grade. A large proportion of the children do not attend school beyond the first year. Even more significant is the fact that half of the children in the rural districts have no schools to go to.

Even in the Federal District where schooling for the children is on everyone's conscience, it is estimated that out of approximately 1,000,000 schoolchildren, between 50,000 to 100,000 have no school to go to. The school population has grown faster than schools could be provided or teachers trained. In the rural districts the situation is even more difficult. President López Mateos, who is seriously concerned about education, has recognized that providing adequate schooling for all of the children is a gigantic undertaking and "it would be illusory to believe that we could accomplish it in the course of a six-year term." [1]

Since 1920 the population of Mexico has more than doubled and the number of children in the population has increased more rapidly than the adults. This has hampered the government's ability to wage an effective campaign for rural schools. It has not been able to train teachers and supply school materials and supervisors in sufficient numbers to make effective headway against illiteracy. This is the story in Mexico, which justly prides itself on its contribution to education and its efforts to meet the challenge of literacy in the modern world.

Although Mexico has made important strides in converting a hacienda-dominated and peon-ridden society into one that is democratic, progressive, and full of confidence in its own future, a careful analysis of what has happened in the last 37 years would probably show that

[1] *The New York Times,* January 18, 1958.

other influences in addition to a rapidly growing population must be reckoned with in explaining the failure of the school system to keep up with the number of children clamoring for schools. One of these factors has undoubtedly been an overemphasis upon urbanization and a tendency to neglect the needs of the rural community, even though Mexico's Revolution of 1910 was primarily a protest against just this kind of neglect. But rural people in Latin America are on the whole voiceless and fail to bring their needs to the attention of the government immersed in the large city.

More fundamental, perhaps, is the simple fact that, in spite of great functional changes, literacy in the rural districts still remains less important than in the cities. If this is the case in a country where the hacienda system has been destroyed and where the impulse toward a fuller democracy is the outstanding feature, what can be said of the rest of Latin America?

One must be on guard against generalizations and dogmatic assertions, and no one really knows enough to be absolutely sure of his own position in matters as complex as this, but it seems obvious that where a country is divided into large haciendas on which a large proportion of the people live, the motivation for organizing and the income to finance an effective system of rural education is lacking. The hacienda is chiefly responsible for the paradox faced by Latin America in its efforts to adapt to modern ways, not only in the matter of schooling for the mass of the people, but also in its efforts to industrialize and apply scientific methods to its agriculture. The paradox lies in the fact that the demand for modernization is made by the very elements who are most insistent on keeping the older social and economic institutions. These people clamor for progress and at the same time resist effective change. They would like to retain their hierarchical, authoritarian, and centralized social structure but also have the values that only come with an egalitarian, mobile, individualistic society, which industrialism both needs and promotes. It is, I think, clear that an effective modern school system would require so many other changes that it can only come into being as the countries develop the resources, the needs, and the competencies which make universal literacy an integral part of a modern society.

4. Higher Education

Higher education in Latin America is going through a profound crisis. The older universities which served a small aristocracy have been challenged to meet the seemingly impossible demands of a suddenly enlarged urban population. A growing middle class and an expanding industrial system, with its emphasis on science and scientific training, demand more than the older universities with their literary traditions, emphasis on the humanities, and specialization in law, medicine, and civil engineering are currently prepared to offer. The sudden flood of students has turned the relatively small traditional institutions of higher learning into great centers of discontent. The universities on the whole lack the means, the trained personnel, the physical plant, and the scientific equipment required to train the thousands of students clamoring for instruction. In addition, students are not always adequately prepared for the university because of inadequate secondary schools. In the majority of cases the professors have made their living by practicing a profession or occupying some post in the government. Their teaching is in a sense an honorific exercise for which they receive a modest, almost a symbolic stipend.

With part-time teaching staffs, inadequate finances, overcrowded halls and classrooms, and poor or nonexistent laboratories, the universities have troubles enough without the added perplexities of involvement with the government. There is, since the University Reform movement which began in Córdoba, Argentina, in 1918, and spread to all of Latin America, a tradition of autonomy and freedom from state interference in university matters. The present rule allows no policeman within the precincts of the university. This autonomy of the university has sometimes led to the conversion of the student body into armed partisans of different political parties, a state within a state.

The ideal of academic inviolability has been frequently disregarded—Venezuela under Pérez Jiménez, Cuba under Batista, and Argentina under Perón provide only the most recent instances of government interference in academic affairs. State intervention on the one hand and students' demands for participation in university administration and policy-making on the other have made academic life exciting, if not entirely peaceful, and devotion to research and the scholarly life difficult. There are many distinguished scholars and teachers who have somehow managed to find the serenity needed for creative work within this difficult environment, but there are also many teachers and students who find the going hard and the rewards inadequate. There are a few private, usually Catholic, universities that are less troubled by politics, but in the broad field of education they differ but little from the nationally supported institutions. If one is to offer a constructive comment on so sensitive a matter as the university in Latin America, it should be done humbly and with many apologies. But it does seem that it is an error to overemphasize and overembellish the university in the capital cities—Lima, Mexico, Caracas—and neglect the smaller regional institutions in Cuzco, Morelia, Quenca, and Popayán. This is but one suggestion. There are many others that an outsider could make. But then an outsider does not understand or have to deal with the ten thousand stumbling blocks which impede any modification of the tradition-bound ways of a university that must continue to live with centralized, authoritarian, and all-powerful government.

CHAPTER 7

LEADERSHIP

1. *The Cosmic Race*

WHEN Latin Americans say—as they often do when speaking of themselves—"We are a young people," they must have in the back of their minds Bolívar's remark that the inhabitants of the former Spanish colonies were neither Europeans, Africans, nor Indians, but Americans. That too was the idea of the "Cosmic Race" popularized by José Vasconcelos a generation ago. These reflections by Latin Americans are a way of saying that the people of Latin America are still being formed, that the "Cosmic Race" is an aspiration, an ideal to be hoped for but at present unrealized. If this means anything, and I think that such intuitive reflections by a people about themselves mean a great deal, it is that the mestizo, who is the product of this amalgam between all the races, has not as yet become the universal type, the true representative of the "Cosmic

Race," and the character of the Latin American has not yet been integrated. For in spite of their sensitivity about criticism from the outside, Latin Americans acknowledge the validity of such critical analysis as Carlos Octavio Bunge's *Our America* (Buenos Aires; 6th ed., 1918) and Luis Alberto Sánchez's *Does Latin America Exist?* (Mexico, D.F.; 1945) and honor these authors for their frankness as well as their wisdom.

The meaning of the statement, "We are a young people," is that the Indians, Negroes, and Europeans still comprise distinct racial groups, while the mestizo, the real American, remains an imperfect creature because he is born and reared amid conflicting values and contradictory cultures. The Englishman, Frenchman, or Italian seems to have basic attitudes that go back beyond the memory of man, and his notions of right and wrong seem to have universal acceptance. The mestizo, on the other hand, is raised in a world where even the most intimate truths are challenged and denied. The Indians and Africans and Europeans among whom he lives differ from each other in their simplest ideas of the good, and each of them differs from the mestizo.

The import of all this is unconsciously revealed when we in the United States ask about any political personage: "Who is he? . . . Where was he born? . . . Where did he go to school?" We ask these questions not because we want to know the man's political opinions—those he has revealed by his party allegiance and by his public statements. The queries go to the heart of the matter. They ask not what the person thinks, but how he came to be the kind of man he is; his opinions about politics are only part of the question.

What kind of a character is he, regardless of his opinions? This question of character formation in a world of conflicting values, beliefs, and ideals has been answered many times and in many places. But an unstable and conflicting cultural environment is not conducive to the formation of the "national" type. Contradictory cultures and differing value systems have nurtured refractory characters, especially among the mestizos, who are "a young people," a people just coming to be. Otherwise it would be difficult to explain the turbulence and instability, the passion and the frustration, the alternatives of pride and humility, of arrogant self-assertion one day and sense of inferiority the next, that are so frequently manifested in Latin American history.

The mestizo is a child of conquest, misfortune, denial, and contempt. Between the conquest, when he did not yet exist, and independence, when he began to emerge as an active participant—at least as a sergeant and sometimes an important leader like Morelos in Mexico—and the present there has not been time for a national culture broad enough to embrace the entire population to emerge. Nor will it emerge until in some way a fusion of the races occurs, bringing with it that condition of common values, that unofficial education in right and good, which precedes any schooling in a traditionally pervasive culture.

This widespread difficulty is clearly seen in Guatemala. Who in Guatemala speaks for all of the people? Culturally, no one. Certainly not the mestizo (*ladino*, as he is called) nor the *criollo* (who here is also called a *ladino*) nor the Indian. The Indian, of course, is voiceless. He does not speak to the public at large. He speaks in a dozen mutually unintelligible tongues and is not really aware of what the Guatemalan nation claims to be. He would prefer to be left alone to go his own way, worshipping God, ordering his civil affairs, dealing with the complexities of family life, and tilling the land as he has always done. How far away and how indifferent to the modern world he can be is illustrated by the day-to-day use, in some Indian villages, of the ancient Mayan calendar to schedule religious activities during the year.

The mestizo who does make himself heard and has taken over the leadership of the government is indifferent if not hostile to the Indian and his ways. The mestizo talks in public and to the world at large as if the Indian did not matter or did not exist. General Jorge Ubico, for so many years the dictator of Guatemala, attempted to deny the Indian's presence to the outside world. In a motion picture of Ubico's accomplishments as president, filmed for distribution in Central America, the Indian was cut out of the picture whenever possible. Wherever Ubico was shown, he managed to be surrounded solely by *ladinos*. Only in one flash did an Indian face and head slip into one very good shot—too good to be cut. Guatemala was to be shown to the world as a mestizo nation, though the Indian is at least one half of the population.

The *criollo*, in Guatemala, has largely lost his identity. There is really no one in the nation who can stand above the conflict of cultures and speak of the body of the nation as one people. If anyone did, he would be driven from office by the mestizos because they represent whatever effective power there is.

It ought to be clear that this is not a matter of conservatism, liberalism, democracy, socialism, communism, or whatever slogan may be in vogue in the next generation. It is the incompatability of two cultures with basically different value systems. The unity that the nationalist aspires to will appear only when the Indian has so completely merged with the mestizo that he is no longer aware of himself. How long it will take no one can tell. But until then, there can be no national leadership because culturally there is no nation.

One can say something very similar about Peru, Ecuador, Mexico before the Revolution of 1910, Bolivia until 1952, and other countries to the extent that they possess nonassimilated Indian groups. It is significant that in the midst of the bitterness and violence of the Mexican revolution, the attitude of thoughtful Mexicans was that they were "making a nation" (*forjando patria*). That is the title Manuel Gamio gave to a book of essays dealing with the Mexican upheaval and published in 1922. It is equally noticeable that the Bolivian intellectuals, after the defeat of their country in the Chaco War, were obsessed with the idea of making a nation and bringing the Indian into the public arena. That perhaps is as good an explanation of the Bolivian revolution as can be found. The question of whom the leader speaks for is a baffling matter everywhere, but particularly so in Latin America.

There are few places in other parts of the world where so great a difference can be found among the "citizens" of the same nation. Culturally most of the nations of Latin America are a kaleidoscope of society, from the most primitive to the most complex, from the naked Amazonian—such as the Auca Indians on the Napo River who recently killed some missionaries because they look upon every white man as an enemy—to the sophisticated intellectual in Quito, Lima, or Mexico City, who reads Sartre and considers himself an existentialist. These societies, occupying the same territory but standing at the extremes of human experience, are more common throughout Latin America than is generally assumed. The Tarahuamara in Chihuahua, the Lacandone in Chiapes, and the forest and jungle people in Brazil, Colombia, and Venezuela are but the end of a line. They are more significant than their numbers would suggest.

We are faced, on the one extreme, with a society whose members have no notion of property and whose basic needs are supplied within some roughly defined area by hunting and fishing, and, on the other, with the intricacies of the modern corporation, perhaps registered in Delaware and doing business through one or more subsidiaries in Peru, Mexico, or Brazil. Within these extremes is every gradation of collective and private ownership. The communal villages in the highlands of western South America range from full collective ownership to villages where the agricultural lands are held by individuals but the pasture lands belong to the community. These different peoples are as much a part of the nation as the mestizos or the *criollos*. Statesmanship would not only require the acceptance of different races, beliefs, and language as equally part of the nation; it would also recognize the great range of custom and law by which these various peoples regulate their conduct toward each other and toward the group of which they are a part. The recognition of unity in variety, of a culture rich in its possibilities because of the unique values and meanings contributed by each of these groups, would be the height of statesmanship. Only José Gervasio Artigas, the inspired leader of the Uruguayan people, had the wisdom and the humility to accept the Indian as he was. "I wish that the Indians in their villages should govern themselves and protect their interests as we do ours." Such leadership is hard to come by.

The assertion that all men are equal is an ancient doctrine, deeply ingrained in Christian culture. This idea gets itself written into the constitutions of Latin America. But the idea that the various cultures within the nation are equally legitimate—that local custom and common law ought to be protected against violence and abuse—has found no Rousseau, even though, in Latin America, the persistent variable in social structure is important historically as well as in the present.

It may be asking too much of national leadership to be sensitive and responsive to the needs and difficulties of all cultural groups. But these groups are the body of the nation in a country like Guatemala. If national leadership is to have any meaning, it ought to be responsive to these groups.

2. *The Mestizo as Leader*

One way of looking at the failure to develop national leadership is to glance at the problem historically.

The Latin American *criollo* had little part in government during the colonial period and lacked business experience. Thus, after the independence and all through the nineteenth century, business and industrial affairs fell by default to Spaniards, Italians, Germans, Englishmen, North Americans, and others. The aristocratic elements who went to the universities either at home or abroad, preferably in France, became doctors and lawyers, and dabbled in literature and, if they stayed at home, in politics. The tradition of the hacienda opposed preoccupation with the material world, with business and industry or even with agriculture. In a sense, the upper classes were oriented toward Europe and indifferent to the problems facing their own country. They were, after all, only a fraction of the total population, and because of the prevailing hierarchical society, they remained "above the battle," lacking the ability, interest, or necessary involvement to take effective hold of the government. They did not possess the *esprit de corps* of a governing class. They were not the natural leaders of the populace. They had not risen from them and they lacked their loyalty and affection. They were not only "above the battle" but so high above the people that the leadership of the nation could not rest in their hands.

By default, the leadership of the nation rested with the mestizo, who had neither the tradition, the education, nor the experience for the task. Basically the mestizo in the nineteenth century was on the make. He used whatever means to power, prestige, and affluence were available to him, with little scruple and no conscience. But as the leader of a faction or a political family, as the *caudillo* of a region, as the "colonel" of the militia, or as an ambitious and likable politically minded officer in the national army he achieved national influence. He was not necessarily a philosopher, a political scientist, or a man of great vision. These qualities were not excluded but they were not a prerequisite. What he needed was audacity, physical courage, indifference to life, great energy, ambition, friends, a family—a political family, *compadres*—a reputation for loyalty, the qualities of a demagogue, and an ability to dazzle his followers by an unexpected trait of some kind. He had to be generous to his immediate followers but offer to and exact from his political family an absolute loyalty.

This leadership was not dependent upon formal political parties, which at the time did not exist. The leader, however, did not stand alone; he had a personal party bound by ties which could not be broken except in death. In Latin America there is always a community, a tradition, a church, or a family in the background. The individual stands inside and not outside of these encompassing influences, as he tends to do in the United States. And in instances where these warming and protective relationships have been weakened in Latin America, they are replaced by an informal but compelling association that stems from having gone to the same school, lived in the same neighborhood, or followed the same leader. These ties have elements of fidelity and identity that will outlast misfortune, poverty, exile, and even crime. Even in sophisticated groups whose main occupation is public service and active participation in politics, there is a tradition of deference to the needs of the in-group that takes precedence over every other consideration. To stand by your group, the members of your extended family, your classmates, those raised with you in the same village, the *compadre,* or your companions who followed the same political leader takes precedence over efficiency, public service, budgetary restrictions, or formal law.

We call it nepotism, favoritism, political irresponsibility, financial mismanagement, or peculation. But that view of the matter assumes that the government is everybody's government rather than "our government"—the government of those in power for the time being. It assumes that a public official could or should disregard in the name of public service the needs and expectancies of relatives, friends, neighbors, and companions, who have lived with him, protected, befriended, and perhaps housed and fed him. It assumes that the abstract thing called "the government" should displace in his affection those who have always filled the days of his life, who came in dozens to see him off when he went on a journey, who gathered and made a festive occasion of his *día de Santo,* who filled the house with laughter and music when he graduated from school, who converted every incident in his life into a symbol of fellowship and identity, and will continue to do so long after he is out of the government.

Relations within the group are permanent. Political office is temporary and precarious and is expected to be so. The public association, the party, the cause (outside of the Church) to which individuals can be attached, does not exist. There are exceptions, of course, such as the Liberals and Conservatives in Colombia, or the Colorados and Blancos in Uruguay. But these are isolated instances. The phenomenon so common in the United States—of lifelong service to a public cause such as the Red Cross, the Civil Liberties Union, the American Prison Association, the Public Library Association, or the Federation of Women's Clubs—is simply nonexistent. The tradition of individualism, the special complex of mestizo society, the sense of insecurity, and the preoccupation with the family in its larger sense have confined and circumscribed the individual within his family clan. But inside that particular association, loyalty and devotion are likely to be lifelong, above both good and evil and fortune.

If this does not provide the best grounds for national leadership, it gives an ideal basis for the perpetuation of local leadership, the survival of the local family, and the persistent influence of regionalism in politics. We have known something of the same sort in our own Southern states. But the Southern states are a minority influence in a highly dynamic society—which is not the case in Latin America. There the closely knit regional political family, clan, gang, party, or whatever name we choose to give it—and none are adequate—is pervasive. All of social and political life has this basis. In the feelings of the people the idea of the region is sharp and distinct, whereas the nation is vague and ephemeral. When we talk about leadership this is the ground upon which it stands. Even in Brazil one is a Paulista, that is, from the state of São Paulo, rather than a Brazilian in a sense that does not exist in the United States, not even among Texans.

In some subtle way these dispersing influences have played an important role in the history of repeated dictatorship. The nation cannot be governed solely in the interest of regional political clans. The national government, however it came to power, has to make its peace with the sectional claimants, with the political gangs—factions, families—that rule the different parts of the country. If the president will not surrender to the splintering influences, and if he lacks the skill to compose and compromise, then dictatorship becomes the inevitable choice. This is not a defense of dictatorship but an attempt to understand why the dictator has played such a conspicuous role in this part of the world.

Another aspect of dictatorship in Latin America is the role of the army. In one respect the army, especially in recent years, is the only secular institution that has had a national outlook and can thus stand above party and region. The case of Argentina's General Aramburu, who held on to the government after the fall of Perón until he could transfer it to an elected president, is illustrative of the point. The government has gone to the army for reasons too numerous to deal with here, but one of these reasons is that the army can see the whole of the nation where other institutionalized forces are only interested in a part of it. Where there is no nationally organized power to challenge the legitimacy of the army's claims to represent or govern the nation, it is no accident that the leaders of the nation have often been soldiers—the nation as a nation has meaning to them.

These are complicated matters that must not be simplified because they may also be falsified in the process. The leadership of the nation requires a symbol, a vision, a policy, and a faith which transcend the particular. But the mestizo to whom leadership has fallen has on the whole neither the tradition nor the training for national leadership—that is, for being the leader of all of the people. There are, of course, many individual exceptions that could be mentioned—Lleras Camargo, Lázaro Cárdenas, José Figueras, etc.—but these men are not typical of the Latin American political leader.

3. The Intellectuals

The only other source of effective leadership in Latin America is the intellectual. The recognized poet, novelist, or historian—but especially poet—has a distinctive place in the affections and regard of his compatriots. The funeral cortege of a well-known literary figure in any of the capitals of Latin America will be followed by thousands of people. Recently something like 30,000 people followed the funeral carriage of a famous Mexican historian.

The literary man is a national figure with an influence independent of government position or party affiliation. This provides him with an admirable and unique basis for asserting national leadership. It is admirable because he is independent, and unique because he cannot be deprived of the following that he has except by ceasing to write and publish. He has another qualification for national leadership not shared by many of his contemporaries. He, more than most, is likely to have a vision of the nation as a whole. He can be above party, region, or class. He will, more than others, have had contact with cultures other than his own and know something of the complexities and difficulties of the world about him, understand something of the possibilities and limits of public policy, and be aware of the temper of the age in which he lives.

To begin with, the intellectuals—and that includes the better-known artists, poets, novelists, historians, and literary critics—were oriented toward Europe, particularly France, rather than their own country. This was generally true until the First World War, and only gradually—and perhaps not completely even today in some sections—have they discovered their own country. It has been accurately pointed out that Brazilian intellectual history can be divided into the period before and the period after the publication of Gilberto Freyre's *Casa Grande y Senzala* (1933; translated as *The Masters and the Slaves*). Until the appearance of this remarkable social history of Brazil, writers were preoccupied with European subjects and paid little attention to their own country or to its problems. When they did, it was to deprecate its backwardness and reflect in sadness upon the mixture of Negro, Indian, and white as something unhealthy if not unnatural, condemning their country to inferiority.

Since the publication of *The Masters and the Slaves,* a flood of volumes have appeared on Brazilian subjects. The great merit of this remarkable book is that it caused Brazilians to discover themselves. Instead of running away from race mixture as a scandal and a shame, they find that their literature, music, art, and architecture has been given vitality and richness through the fusion of races and cultures. They consider Brazil a model for the world to follow and Brazilian culture as a uniquely rich contribution to civilization. *Casa Grande y Senzala* has the special merit of having changed Brazil's image of itself in one generation.

Something similar occurred in Mexico following the revolution, and especially after the Cárdenas regime, which greatly increased Mexican dignity and self-respect. It was during this period that Mexico stopped living in constant fear of the United States. The Mexicans like the Brazilians have accepted themselves as they are. They are not Europeans or North Americans and do not wish to be. They have a sense of importance and pride in the vast outpouring of energy that has gone into their new art and architecture, their music and poetry, and now their fiction and drama. And all of this is Mexican. It is, I think, admittedly clear that Diego Rivera and Clemente Orozco could only be Mexicans, and that no other people could have built the Mexican National University. Mexicans are no longer ashamed of having Indian blood in their veins and no longer drive the Indians from the main streets. But in both Brazil and Mexico this facing of the national reality is too recent to have allowed for a couple of generations to grow to intellectual maturity free from the sense of being culturally outcast. A maturity evidenced in self-confidence without self-consciousness is a prerequisite for the development of leadership in a nation, whether it is drawn from among the intellectuals or not.

Beyond Brazil and Mexico, however, where does one find this kind of intellectual revolution? Latin American intellectuals have been immersed for so long in European models that they have, in most places, barely escaped them. There is obvious danger in overstating this proposition, and I can hear vigorous disclaimers from Argentinians, Colombians, Uruguayans, and Costa Ricans, but as an outsider and a friendly one, I can only say that the willingness to accept oneself and live with oneself that has come as something of a miracle to Brazil and Mexico has not occurred in other countries—certainly not in Peru, Bolivia, Ecuador, Venezuela, or Guatemala, to mention only a few. Without this acceptance of the nation as it is, effective leadership is impossible.

There are other stumbling blocks in the path of the intellectual's aspiration to national leadership. By tradition, training, and family (until very recently indeed) he has belonged to the aristocracy. He is within and not outside the authoritarian and hierarchical fellowship. His contacts are not with the people, and until very recently indeed, what he knew about the people came from sociologists, political scientists, and philosophers published in

Europe, writing about European problems or about other parts of the world, from a European point of view. Only in this generation, more accurately only since the Second World War, have universities attempted to organize research courses in the fields of the social sciences and economics. To this day, however, these courses are limited to a relatively small number of institutions and are inadequately staffed.

Intellectuals interested in dealing with important questions of politics, government, economic growth, business organization, finance, taxation, unemployment, and social security—with any one of the questions that contemporary society has to deal with—had to go to foreign books or foreign universities. Fundamentally, there was little local intellectual interest in these matters. The intellectual tradition was literary and theoretical. European postulates in sociology, politics, economics, and philosophy were absorbed with avidity, as were the doctrines of positivism, syndicalism, socialism, communism, and existentialism, but they were taken over as ideas rather than as policies or programs. Traditionally, intellectual attitudes had little to do with actual political programs or social policy.

The centralized character of government, the habit of expecting the government to do whatever had to be done, and the overwhelming impact of the aristocratic, authoritarian, and hierarchical view of things really meant that ideas were things to argue about or play with—not the basis for formulating programs or policies. Even when ideas such as democracy or federalism got into constitutions—as the history of the last century and a half illustrates—they remained ideas rather than norms of conduct. More recently, elaborate provisions on human rights and civil liberties have been written into state documents, but these too have too often remained merely ideas rather than implemented codes of behavior. A theory like democracy, communism, socialism, or whatnot has to make its way in a milieu where older and deeper attitudes, without formal doctrine but nonetheless very real, elicit primary allegiance. The fact is that the Latin American is a humanist rather than a materialist. His society is compassionate rather than egalitarian, authoritarian rather than democratic. It does not understand that authority is divisible, that the president can be defeated by Congress or flouted by the court and still remain president. It does not understand that other institutions besides government can exercise important public functions. The Latin American attitude is one of acquiescence to the protective power of the mighty one as long as the mighty one does no violence to basic traditions, and if he does, willingness to destroy his power by revolution and replace him.

Basically, Latin Americans would protect the poor, save their dignity, relieve pain, and assuage sorrow rather than reform, change, improve, or upset status, position, belief, or ideals. To most Latin Americans the reformers are following strange gods. In spite of their many revolutions, they are neither revolutionary nor radical. Their revolutions attempt to re-establish an older ideal society, hierarchical and authoritarian, compassionate and sensitive to human dignity—even of the lowest, of the peon—rather than to overthrow it. The rebellious nationalism so much in evidence is not against authoritarianism or hierarchy but against the cold materialism of modern industrialism, so preoccupied with efficiency that it takes from men what they most value—their dignity.

4. The Schizophrenic World

This is perhaps a good place to say a few words about American enterprise in Latin America. The objection to American enterprise is not that it is American but that it is efficient, purposeful, direct, single-minded, and materialistic. In the Latin American culture, business is a part of the total scheme of things: it is part of the family, of the *compadre* relation, of friendships, and of the Church. Business is done among friends in a leisurely and understanding way. Material success is at the bottom of the scale. First of all comes the protection of the family, the *compadres,* the friends. Every relationship, no matter how unimportant in business, is important on the human side, for each man must be treated with courtesy and dignity, almost as a member of the family. The efficiency and single-mindedness of American enterprise is unaware of, or indifferent to, this scheme of ethical and aesthetic values. Its very egalitarianism and familiarity are offensive to the Latin American. It is conspicuously different, not because it is American or foreign, but because its scheme of values is different.

American enterprise cannot identify with the aristocratic agrarian tradition or with the growing middle class. To the first it is a threat; to the second it seems a block in their own path, especially since the foreign corporation has not, until recently, offered the young middle class or the young intellectuals an outlet for their ambitions. It has not given them, or is believed not to have given them, equality of opportunity within the administration. In the United States a new industry means new opportunities for advancement. In Latin America a new foreign enterprise has often meant the exclusion of locally competent young people of good families. Neither the business community nor the intellectuals find this congenial. Their life is involved in the total culture, while the American businessman or manager stands outside their culture and is somehow beyond their reach. They have no way of bending the new enterprise to their older values, no way of losing themselves within the new venture, and no way of denying its irritating presence.

Americans are not particularly helpful in this. They do not ordinarily associate with the members of their host community, and when they do, their patronizing attitude adds nothing to their good standing. Americans usually live by themselves and do not participate in the affairs of the community. In an active industrial region where some hundreds of American university-trained specialists in many fields were located, the rector of the university was asked whether any of this highly select group of Americans took any interest or part in the many activities of this university. He replied: "These people do not associate with us."

If one searches into the reason for the hostility shown to Mr. Nixon in 1958, here is one key. In the complaints raised by intellectuals against American imperialism, economic and even political arguments, though often used, are of secondary importance—they are part of the contemporary fashion in public debate. The deeper grievance —that Americans are oblivious to and disdainful of Latin American values and a sense of personal dignity—is more difficult to express and much too painful to cry in the marketplace.

American business and American policy have been guilty of obtuseness and insensitivity. No amount of good will, back-slapping, or offers of material aid are adequate substitutes for understanding and being sensitive to the values that give meaning and direction to life itself. Our efficiency and purposefulness, our "go-getterness," and our enthusiasm for material success prove most irritating and incomprehensible to the Latin American. If only we were less in a hurry, less bent on getting things done quickly, if only we had time for talk and friendliness and courtesy, if only we did not seem to push people around and in our haste forget or be ignorant of the amenities essential to friendly relations. As one Latin American expressed it: "Our greatest difficulties are over little, seemingly unimportant things."

The Latin American intellectuals—students, professors, artists, writers, and poets—have found American "crudities," as they would call them, so frustrating that on occasion they have been prepared to say: "Keep your good will, your material offerings, and your bad manners. We will have none of them." These things are hard to say and difficult to write about. One of the most intelligent and best-known Latin American historians—friendly to the United States and an open enemy of Communism—once remarked: "In all of my experience I have never known an American representative who was either a gentleman or a scholar. Why is it that the older tradition of sending distinguished writers and scholars as ministers and ambassadors has so completely disappeared?" Fortunately President Kennedy has brought the scholar and writer back into public and diplomatic life and given them an opportunity to play an important part in contemporary affairs.

It is important to keep in mind that these feelings and attitudes, so frequently voiced, if muted, are not confined to one country. Latin America may be divided into 20 separate nations, but intellectually it is very much one community. Many of its most distinguished contemporary writers are almost household names among the literate people in the entire area, particularly in the Spanish-speaking countries. These include the late Alfonso Reyes (whose death was mourned all over Latin America) from Mexico, Germán Arciniegas from Colombia, Picón Salas and Rómulo Gallegos from Venezuela, Luis Alberto Sánchez from Peru, Gilberto Freyre from Brazil, Luis Romero from Argentina, Fernando Ortiz from Cuba, and others.

The influence of the intellectuals reaches far beyond their native borders. Partly this is due to the tradition of writing syndicated articles which appear in both large and small newspapers throughout Latin America. One can find an article by Germán Arciniegas, Luis Alberto Sánchez, Alfonso Reyes, etc., printed in *El Excelsior* in Mexico, *El Tiempo* in Bogotá, *La Prensa* in Argentina, *El Comercio* in Quito, in fact in all of the countries and in most of the cities that have papers of their own. These articles are often serious literary productions. Books written by these scholars are published in relatively inexpensive paper editions and circulate over the whole area. Sometimes such books can be found in bookstores in little towns like Otawala in Ecuador. Not infrequently, the intellectuals have taught in the universities of more than one country and have served as ambassadors or ministers. It is customary to send such distinguished literary figures to represent their countries in foreign posts. Picón Salas has served in Colombia and in Brazil; Alfonso Reyes represented Mexico in Rio de Janeiro; Germán Arciniegas in Argentina and Rome; etc. This is worth noting in contrast to our own practice. It is a long time since a Lowell represented the United States in Spain or an Adams in England. President Kennedy's appointments are a welcome reversal of what had become traditional American policy—that no intellectual should occupy a diplomatic post.

Many of these intellectuals, exiled from their own land, have lived in other Latin American countries where they have usually been treated with the greatest consideration and friendliness. Therefore in spite of the wide dispersal of the capitals of Latin America and their meager economic contacts, the intellectuals have always inhabited a community that embraced all of Latin America. An adverse or favorable opinion of the United States, a criticism of a book, or the expression of an individual judgment on some question of public policy will automatically receive attention and be commented upon in the public press over a continent and a half.

Whatever nationalism there may be in other fields, the Latin Americans live intellectually in the same community. This is illustrated in many ways. A small weekly journal was published and printed in San José, Costa Rica, for many years by a single individual, García Monge, who did all the work himself. It never had a large circulation by newspaper standards, but it was known and cherished by the most influential intellectuals in each country. A single contribution to *El Repertorio* would establish a young writer's continental reputation. Something similar may be said about Victoria Ocampo's literary journal *Sur*, published in Argentina. Much more literary and sophisticated, and much closer to French and general European literary influence, this journal, too, is more than a local magazine published in Buenos Aires. But the most remarkable evidence of a common intellectual community is *Cuardernos Americanos*, published in Mexico by Silva Hertzog. This quarterly circulates over all of Latin America, and is perhaps the standard opinion-making literary journal. There is nothing so well written or so wide in its interests printed in the United States, and perhaps not anywhere else. Its writers are drawn from all the countries, and its pages are open to literary excellence regardless of the subject—it will print serious discussion on poetry, philosophy, physics, history, international affairs, or whatever. In some ways it is the symbol of Latin American unity that the intellectuals are always talking about. It is often anti-American, but so are many of the intellectuals in Latin America.

The United States government, therefore, is not dealing with a single country even when it is presumably talking only to the Minister of Nicaragua or of Argentina. Vis-à-vis the United States, there is a community of public opinion which is as wide as the continent and includes all of the nations south of the American border. In many things there are sharp differences among these nations and even bitter antagonism. But concerning the United States there is wide agreement on many matters; on some there is well nigh unanimity. And to no small degree this is the work of the intellectuals. Not only have the intellectuals been leaders in molding a Latin American community, at least on the intellectual level, but indirectly they have also had great influence on the political attitudes of their communities toward the United States. In some ways the intellectuals have been more influential as leaders of the continental community than of their own particular countries, for, except in Colombia, they have rarely achieved actual political power. They are the moderators, critics, gadflies, and opponents, but not the political leaders, although they are often influential in shaping the public opinion that determines who comes to office and what policies will be pursued. The realities of the situation require us to recognize that the intellectuals are neither willing nor able to face the schizophrenic world they live in. They value greatly all that a "patronal" and aristocratic society has given them—the ease, the unhurried life, the indifference to great wealth, the presence of many servants to make life comfortable and secure, the romantic notion of a heroic past and the encouragement of friendships and versatility. All of this they would keep. But they also want, or think they want, what the modern world has to offer—modern cities, automobiles, airplanes, factories, the latest products of science, and the gadgets of the day. They would have the best of two worlds—the patronal, *señorial* society and the egalitarian and industrial one— and refuse to recognize that they cannot have both.

There is no way out of this dilemma by a deliberate act of will. The intellectuals cannot reject either of the two worlds or remain content with one. The schizophrenic world they live in is beyond their control. We must recognize that for the next generation or longer the intellectuals will be restless, bitter, and turbulent. The United States will be the major target of their inability to square the circle, to make an agrarian feudalism fit in nicely with an industrial egalitarianism. Fortune has cast the United States as the major symbol of their dissatisfaction with both worlds.

CHAPTER 8

POLITICS

1. *"The Political Party"*

POLITICS in this world we have been describing is very
"political," very "pragmatic," and not at all "ideological."
It is also very personal.

I remember many years ago, on a train from Vera Cruz
to Mexico City, talking to a Honduran military man going
into exile. "How many political parties are there in Honduras?" I asked.

"Only two: the Red and the Green. I belong to the Green
Party," he replied.

"And what is the difference between them?"

After a moment's reflection he said: "Well, there is really
no difference between them, only naturally I think that
the Green Party is better."

I didn't in those days know enough about Latin America

to appreciate the profound political lesson I had just been given. For what this man was trying to tell me was the simple and profound truth that Latin American politics were not ruled by theoretical considerations, that political parties were neither left nor right, but that they were good or bad depending upon whether they belonged to us or to our opponents. If the party belonged to us, it was good. If it belonged to our opponents, it was bad. Political differences were real enough but not for ideological reasons.

This is an oversimplification of the complexities of the political process in Latin America, but it is one way of saying that politics, political parties, and government administrations are personal. "Personal" here means that the government belongs to the successful leader because the political party belongs to him, and because the members of the party are also his or they would not belong to his party. The important political consideration is the leader and not the party.

There have been changes in Latin America in the last generation which have complicated and obscured the political scene without really changing its character. The spread of doctrines such as Nazism, fascism, socialism, and communism and their adoption as party names have given foreigners and even some culturally Europeanized nationals the impression that something strange has happened in Latin American politics, that what had always been a personal phenomenon has become a matter of ideals, with the party and the ideology displacing the individual, the slogan more important than the leader, the law of greater significance than personal influence, and matters of principle taking precedence over friendship, family, and political clan. Those who have let themselves believe all this have simply lost their bearings and are reading their politics out of a European book.

The one thing that has not changed has been the *caudillo*, the leader, he who has *"la suma del poder,"* who governs because he can, not because he was elected. There were many differences between Fidel Castro and Trujillo, but they had one thing in common. They governed because they could. The fact that Trujillo had himself elected and always received 100 per cent of the vote while Fidel Castro has had no election is irrelevant except as embroidery, or something that gives apparent sanction and satisfies critics in the United States or England who do not really appreciate what is going on. But what is going on has always gone on—if not "always," then at least for a very long time. Leadership is personal. The basis of authority is customary rather than constitutional. The political unit is not the individual; it is the gang, the extended family, the community, and the Indian village, each with its own "natural" leader, each endowed with unlimited authority and each possessing the complete loyalty of his immediate followers.

The great leader, by some magic, fraud, or force, has at his disposal all this power, and he cannot divide it, delegate it, or refuse to use it. As a matter of simple fact, he cannot resign it—as Fidel Castro couldn't resign from being the "maximum leader of the revolution" in Cuba. Castro could resign his office of Premier, but not his personal authority. The *caudillo* governs by his mere presence. Anything he says is an order, and if he refuses to say anything at all, then others will act in his name on the assumption that they are carrying out the orders he would have given, and he will be credited with them. The king could abdicate in favor of the legitimate heir to the Crown. But in Latin America the leader cannot abdicate because there is no legitimate heir to his power. When the successor appears, the power of the older leader evaporates. When Cárdenas came on the scene, the seemingly unbounded power of Calles simply vanished. The power cannot be shared. It is absolute or it does not exist. The belief that Castro's declaring himself a Communist means that a Communist Party will take over his power is something that has to be established. It would prove something that seems incredible to most Latin Americans— that political power can be impersonal.

We have no model for this type of political leadership— although Huey Long of Louisiana came close to it—and therefore we do not understand it. The American gang represents personal leadership which has elements comparable to the *caudillo*. A better comparison is the Scottish clan. The clan was more important than the state and more important than the king. Loyalty was to the clan chieftain first and the clan would follow its leader against other clans, against the king, and against the whole world. But this example, too, is unsatisfactory because chieftainship in the clan was hereditary whereas leadership in Latin America is not.

The case of Fidel Castro is particularly revealing. Cuba is not typical of Latin America. The Indian influence is nil. The Negro, on the other hand, is important in numbers, but even more so in over-all influence. The Negro has given the Cubans a gentle, friendly, and optimistic attitude toward life. They tend to emphasize the importance of the moment. Their land is filled with music, song, and the dance. Also Cuba is close to the United States and our impact upon Cuba has been great—greater, perhaps, than either of us realize. There are, therefore, many reasons for arguing that politically Cuba should be less Latin American than it has shown itself to be. For what it has shown in Fidel Castro is that it still prefers to have a *caudillo*—one who stands above the law and the constitution because all authority, all justice, all good emanates directly from him.

The differences between Fidel Castro and Batista are many and great. But as administrators they both respond to the same demand in the same way. Batista was secretive, cruel, and selfish and acted for himself and a small clique. He depended upon the police and the army, but his power was absolute. All constitutional formulas were secondary. Fidel Castro uses the radio, television, and the secret police. The way things have gone, Castro differs from Batista in his claim that he is the first Cuban to stand for social justice and a strong free Cuba. The uses the power is put to are different, but the exclusive possession of it in a single hand is the same.

The power is put to different use because the individual leaders are different and not because the "party" which carried them to power is different. In fact, there was no party in either Batista's or Fidel Castro's case. The Cuban people accepted Fidel Castro because they wanted him. They had Batista because they tolerated him—even perhaps, until the last two years, wanted him—not because he was "good" or constitutional, but because he was strong, because he was a *caudillo*. If they finally overthrew him—and the active fighters against him were never very numerous—it was because he had become a tyrant, because he was misusing his power beyond reason and beyond the wide tolerance of human fallibility so characteristic of Latin America. He lost what moral sanction he might have had or claimed. His overthrow was accepted as good and the leader of the new revolution was greeted with an outpouring of public joy.

It is difficult for people in the United States to understand why Latin American governments are so unstable, revolutions so numerous, tyrannies so frequent and, occasionally, so bloody and heartless. The ideal of constitutional government has remained an unsatisfied aspiration. This has been true for nearly 150 years, and there is little evidence that Latin America is closer to representative democracy now than it was in the nineteenth century. There are exceptions to these broad generalizations, but the exceptions are few and need to be qualified.

If this had been written in 1920, one exception would have been Argentina. It was taken for granted in Argentina, as well as beyond its borders, that arbitrary dictatorships, military rebellions, and *caudillismo* were a thing of the past. The country prided itself on its difference from the rest of Latin America. It considered itself European, progressive, and democratic. Now we know better.

The rebellion in September 1930, led by General José F. Uriburu, was but the preview of what was to come. The Perón domination of Argentina from 1946 to 1955 demonstrated that Argentina was inside the Latin American political milieu after all. In fact, Perón claimed to build upon a national tradition of personal dictatorship. He evoked the ghost of Juan Manuel Rosas (1792–1877) whose 20-year rule (1829–31, 1835–52) provides a classic example of arbitrary personal power. In fact, there are few cases, even in Latin America, of so deft and so deliberate an exploitation of the ability to charm and frighten people into absolute submission. Rosas's secret agency, the *majorca*, slit the throats of his enemies while followers nourished his ego by exhibiting his portrait in all public places. Even the churches had to accept the portraits of Rosas and place them conspicuously at the altar.

Argentina has this in her background. Rosas is accepted by most historians as a providential, if not as a gracious or kindly, instrument of national unity. The fact that Rosas had been possible made Perón also possible, perhaps inevitable.

Again, if one had been writing in 1930 or even as late as 1940, it would have been impossible to conjure into existence the figure of Samuel Sustado Rojas Pinilla. Certainly most Colombians, as well as the vast majority of foreign students, believed that Colombia had become a model of political stability and constitutional democracy. Yet here, as in Argentina, it proved possible to subvert its political institutions and impose an arbitrary and bloody rule upon the country that lasted, if we include the government of Laureano Gómez, its immediate predecessor, from 1950 to 1957. We cite these instances to suggest that there seems to be a general political pattern in Latin America and that the exceptions may be temporary and require qualification.

The pattern of dictatorship and rebellion, followed again by dictatorship, has not materially changed since 1900. Anyone who would make a count of the abortive uprisings and the successful rebellions in the last 50 years would convince himself that if matters have changed politically, the change has not necessarily been in the direction of greater stability. This is so in spite of an almost universal commitment to the ideals of democracy and constitutional government among Latin American intellectuals and statesmen. Students, scholars, newspapermen, and politicians have written an impressive public record in their striving for political democracy. Every constitution describes in detail the manner in which popular governments are to come to power, how long they are to last, and how they are to be succeeded by another administration freely elected and resting upon the consent of the governed. Up to the present, however, public agitation and constitutional mandate have proved ineffective. Nor is it easy to see how agitation for an ideal representative democracy can be made to enhance political stability. Obviously there is a gap between the democratic ideal aimed at by the reformers and the practical politics of actual government.

The contrast between what men say they want politically and what they do cannot be ascribed to malice or perfidy. That would be too simple. If the political difficulties were merely the product of evil intent, they could be dealt with. Politically active people in Latin America are on the whole neither better nor worse than their kind in other parts of the world. The trouble lies somewhere else. Politicians do what they do because they have only limited alternatives, and it is not always clear that choices other than those they make would always be better.

The social and cultural matrix within which Latin America's political leaders operate at present is such that effective and representative popular democracy is, with few exceptions, not a feasible alternative. The only really responsible question that the democratically minded observer can ask of a politician in Latin America today is whether his conduct is conducive toward increasing the prospect of popular and representative democracy. An honest man would find it difficult to give an honest answer. For how can one be sure that the professed idealist, in his enthusiasm for reform, in his stirring the passions and hopes of simple folk beyond his own ability to satisfy them, may not be sowing the dragon's teeth for some conscienceless tyrant who will make the same promises and fulfill none?

The business of government is to govern. That is the first responsibility. If it fails at that, then the politicians in office will flee the country, seeking exile in places where they will find no relentless responsibilities to fulfill. But to govern in Latin America is an unusually difficult matter.

General Lázaro Cárdenas once remarked that the people of Mexico must learn that they can be governed without violence. Cárdenas, however, had qualities of leadership which made violence unnecessary and governed Mexico that way. But no one else had been able to do so before him. Violence has been an essential fact in Latin America because the governments have been unstable, and the governments have been unstable because violence is a traditional means of coming to office. Violence is traditional because there generally has been no other sure means of transferring political power from one administration to another. This is the heart of the matter: how to come to power without violence and how to transfer power without revolution.

2. The Principle of Legitimacy

In other parts of the world where this political miracle of entering upon and leaving public office in peace is accomplished, there is some universally accepted principle of legitimacy. The transfer of political authority from one administration to another in peace and quiet needs to be symbolized by something which is universally respected and believed in. Such a universal symbol makes the government of today just as legitimate as the government of yesterday in spite of the complete change-over in personnel. "The king is dead—long live the king!" is a perfect example of this kind of symbol of authority. As long as the accepted principle of descent is adhered to, there is never any question as to where authority resides and to whom the crown descends. The government is never without a recognized head. Everyone knows who the king is. No such universally accepted symbol exists in Latin America.

During the colonial period there was no question of where legitimate power resided. The king was the king in all things and at all times. People might have had notions about the wisdom, the stupidity, or even the lunacy of the king or queen, but none about the legitimacy of the power exercised by the king, and the king had no competitors. So universal was this acceptance that it seemed like a part of nature itself. Men laid down their lives for

"God and the King" for so many generations that the "divine" authority of the king was beyond question. The king filled every political and civil need. The king's law protected the innocent and punished the guilty. All offices, all honors, all men, all property, all life itself, were under his protection and held by his mercy.

Even the Church, because of the *patronato*, was, in many important ways, subject to the king. The authority of the crown was everywhere, unquestioned and unopposed. The two things that were known even to the most humble were the power of the king and the mercy of the Lord. Therefore it was always simple to transfer power as long as the rules of succession were followed. The future king was known while the present king was still alive.

It is at this point that the independence movement served the people of Latin America poorly. It destroyed legitimate political power without providing an equally legitimate substitute. When the wars of independence were over, no one knew where political power resided. Who was the legitimate heir to the king of Spain—to his authority, influence, prestige, and semi-sacred character? Who was the embodiment of the will of the people, the protector of the poor, and the fountainhead of justice?

The answer, of course, is that no one inherited those qualities of popularly endowed eminence. No one received the same degree of devotion from the populace and no one was looked to as the unquestioned protector and father of his people. The people of Latin America were left without a legitimate symbol of political authority. That vacuum has remained unfilled to this day.

The absence of the king has not been replaced by "democracy," "federalism," "socialism," "communism," "justicialism," or anything else. Nationalism comes closer than any other "ism" to being a substitute for the idea of the king, but it is relatively recent in Latin America, where many of the nations lack cultural unity. A considerable part of the population, the majority perhaps, in Guatemala, Peru, Bolivia, and Ecuador, for instance, have but the vaguest notion of what the nation means.

There is another difficulty. Nationalism has taken an anti-foreign turn and has become a slogan for demagogues and ambitious politicians. More serious, however, is the absence of a fixed system for deciding who is to represent the nation and how he is to be chosen.

The constitution has proved ineffectual as a means to regulate political behavior. There have been too many constitutions and they have changed too often. Ecuador, for instance, had 16 constitutions in the first 115 years of its national history. They have been disregarded with such regularity that they do not serve to discipline political behavior. When President Rómulo Betancourt of Venezuela presented the constitution written under his auspices, he felt it necessary to assure his nation-wide radio audience that this was a real constitution, not just another little yellow book. In fact, the constitution has too often been a personal political broadside used by the new *mandatario* as his own private declaration and, being private, never meant to be scrupulously followed. What ought to be protected and guarded as the embodiment of all public law and public will has become a matter to be changed, modified, suspended, or abolished. What might have become an effective symbol of authority and a substitute for the awe-inspiring bearer of the Spanish Crown has been perverted to personal use.

An American scholar tells the story that when, as a young man, he went to Venezuela to study its constitutional history, people in Caracas, when they learned of his purpose, said: "Why, he must be a poet." The constitution in their mind had a literary and conceivably a theoretical interest, but certainly not a political one. The scholar finally classified the 19 constitutions as Bolívarian, Conservative, Radical, Federalist, Centralist, and Personalist, and found three constitutions which he could only describe as unclassifiable. All of this merely underlines the point that what does not in fact exist— namely, a recognized basis of political authority, universally accepted and universally respected—cannot be symbolized. This, however, is only one part of the difficulty.

Independence abolished the monarchy but retained what is natural to a monarchy—centralism, authoritarianism, and aristocracy—mainly because the revolutionists were themselves reared in the Spanish tradition and knew no other. Centralism, authoritarianism, and aristocracy were a part of life itself and could not be done away with, since no other way was known either to the leaders or the people.

Following independence, aristocracy disappeared only to the degree that the Spanish aristocrats departed. But the local *criollo* with his claims to nobility remained, and below him were the merchants, farmers, mestizos, *castas,* free Negroes, Negro slaves, and Indians. To all appearances, nothing had changed socially except that a few mestizos had worked their way to public notice by their part in the War of Liberation and a number of Negro slaves had been freed because they had been drafted into the revolutionary armies. Beyond that, the hierarchical structure survived more or less intact in most places throughout most of the nineteenth century and, in some, to the middle of the twentieth.

Natural to the hierarchical structure was the survival of authoritarianism and administrative centralization. The existence of slavery, the survival of Indian peonage, the universality of the hacienda, and the important role of the military all contributed to the maintenance of a political system which did not know how to share or divide authority.

The contrast between an authoritarian and a democratic society lies at this point. A democratic society finds it natural and logical to divide and distribute political authority in many places. No one person or institution is possessed of all the authority of the state. In an authoritarian society, quite the contrary is the case. Political authority is indivisible. The king had *la suma del poder*. In the Latin American republics the president has *la suma del poder*. In Colombia not so long ago I remarked to a friend in high office that I was not so sure about Colombia but that in other countries in Latin America the chief executive had *"todo el poder en sus manos."* He replied: "Here too." The president is *todo poderoso*—all-powerful.

The president has no heir. There is no effective machinery in most countries for transferring political power.[1] This is the most serious crisis facing the elected chief executive. If he does not decide who the next president is

[1] Chile, Costa Rica, Brazil, and Uruguay could be cited as exceptions to this broad generalization, but there are instances in their history during the last 30 years which would make one hesitant about declaring them beyond the tradition of political convulsion. The nation that comes closest to this ideal is probably Uruguay.

going to be, someone will make that decision for him. The outgoing president will soon discover that all of his power has ebbed away to the man who picked the next president. The prospects are that a revolution will be inevitable unless the occupant of the presidential chair is completely pliant. There is a story in Mexico about Ortiz Rubio, which does not have to be true to be important. The fact that it could be told and believed is sufficiently revealing of the political process in an authoritarian and centralized tradition. It is said that Ortiz Rubio heard on good authority that General Plutarco Elías Calles was starting a revolution against him. Ortiz Rubio called General Calles on the phone to inform him that he, the president, was going to join the revolution against the government.

Even if the president does name his successor, he still has the prospect of revolution against his decision. He can be accused of imposing the next president against the will of the people. Where there is no institutionalized and universally acknowledged basis of public power, violence becomes a "natural" means to public office.

In the Spanish tradition, however, political authority must have a moral basis. Power over other people is something that can only be exercised if it has divine sanction. Otherwise it cannot be considered legitimate. Violence is not the route to legitimacy, even if it is successful. The dictator, even when in office, even when he imposes obedience by terror and cruelty, will be held to have no moral basis for his authority. That explains why dictators and others who have come to office by violence continue to hold staged elections as a means of legitimizing their power. In this regard it is interesting to observe that not only did General Rafael Leonidas Trujillo Molina hold

regular elections, but, as has been noted, he saw to it
that at each election he and all of his candidates received
100 per cent of all the votes cast, and not one less. The
old saying that the will of the people is the voice of God
is here taken literally, even if the will of the people has
to be invented before it can be recorded. But such instances, and they are numerous if not as extreme as in
Santo Domingo, merely illustrate that even the tyrant
seeks a moral basis of power.

An Ecuadorian historian writes that from the time of
independence up to 1956 Ecuador had 37 constitutional
chiefs of state, including those re-elected. Of these elections only five have been free. In most of the others the
chief of state had himself elected by an *ad hoc* assembly
called into being for that very purpose by the man who
had overthrown the previous government by violence and
now sought the appearance of legitimacy.

The dictator may be obeyed overtly, but he will be opposed secretly on the grounds that his power is illegiti-
mate, immoral, and tyrannical. The opposition may ultimately triumph, as it did in Venezuela, Argentina, Colombia, and Cuba, but as soon as the revolution is over and
the tyrant is no more, the old dilemma reappears. "The
king is dead. Who is the king now?"

Who shall be the next? Not a tyrant; surely not a dictator. Will the next executive be one who will exercise *lu
suma del poder* but remain a democrat? Will he be a gentle human being who holds all the power of government
without restraint and without limit, but will not use it?
The president cannot divide his authority or delegate it.
The populace will not permit that. The president must be
president. On that point there is general agreement. But

on what grounds does he become president? How does he achieve power? How does he retain it? What is his mandate? To whom is he responsible? There is really no answer to these questions because there is no institutional basis for the political process. There is no absolute rule which determines how the candidate for the highest office comes to be nominated, how, once nominated, he is to be elected, and how, once elected, he is to remain in office for the period set by the constitution. Nor is there anything absolute and sacred about how and to whom he is to transmit power when his legal term of office draws to a close. These questions were faced recently in Argentina, Colombia, Venezuela, and Cuba. In none of them is the answer irrevocable, nor is the occupant of the highest office secure in his post. Even less secure is his ability to transfer the power of his position at the end of his term without a revolution. Pérez Jiménez, Rojas Pinilla, and Batista—all came to office by overthrowing the previous government by a *golpe de estado,* and the ability of the present holders of office who displaced them to pass their power to designated successors is not at all certain. How precarious the tenure of office is can be seen at a glance.

In Argentina the question of whether President Frondizi should be allowed to serve his full term was determined in the negative by the military. In Venezuela the arbiter of the political fortunes of Betancourt is again the army. In both instances the army overthrew the previous regime and occupied the highest office until a civilian could take over.

The case in Colombia is different in the sense that the revolution was made by the people while the army remained neutral. But again an army junta took over office until a civilian could be chosen. In this case an agreement, written into the constitution, for the Liberal and Conservative parties to serve alternate terms in the presidency changes an old tradition that each party had to win power on its merits. The staying power of this arrangement is dubious, despite the successful election of Guillermo León Valencia last May (1962). It still has twelve years to run. Both the Liberal and Conservative parties have split on the question of abiding by these amendments to the constitution, and the alternative is civil war.

The Cuban answer to the question is the emergence of a popular *caudillo* in place of a military dictator. But none of the solutions is perhaps more than transitional. None of them has an institutional basis such as an effective and representative political party system would provide.

3. *The Caudillo*

In the absence of a political party system with roots in local government, the president must be his own party and maintain himself in office by his own ingenuity and political skill, by dependence upon the loyalty of his immediate followers, by compromise, blandishment, and, if these fail him, by force and fraud. What this really means is that the president is not only the chief executive, but also the most active politician, almost the only politician. Under the circumstances no one but the president may be allowed to have political influence.

Where the survival of the administration is in daily question, politics is the act of keeping your political enemies from depriving you of the presidency. What is really involved is not your policy but your power. When the power of the government is so tenuous, the government must do everything because every public act, no matter how small, has political significance, and no one but the president can indulge in activities that have political implications.

Any activity which the president does not control is a threat to his influence and power. He can only have power if he has all the power. If any escapes him, all of it will slip from him because his power is not institutionalized. It belongs to him personally. He must be the whole government—executive, legislative, and judicial. Never mind what the constitution says. The constitution is not the instrument of government. It is only the name in which government is carried on. The president must be his own head of the army, his own cabinet, and, in these days of planning, he must be his own planner. There is no effective political party. There are only the president and his friends, and his friends must be people who will take orders and do what they are told.

The tradition of centralization and the absence of effective party organization define the role of political leadership. The leader must do everything. He must have the answer to all problems and the remedy for every ill. He must accept every responsibility and relieve or promise to relieve every difficulty. José Antonio Páez once wrote Bolívar:

> I do not know why but the people bring me all their problems, how to build a house, whom to

marry, how to settle a family dispute, and what seeds to plant.

He was their leader because they turned to him in need, and expected to be listened to and helped. If he had refused to listen he would soon have lost his leadership. General Lázaro Cárdenas used to spend many hours listening to the poor and humble and make notes of their requests.

Government is personal, intimate, a matter between friends, a family affair. It has to be that way. The people will permit no subordinate to usurp the powers of president, which can only belong to the real leader—the Father. This attitude is pervasive and overrides any party or constitutional thesis that may be professed. This personal dependence upon the leader reduces the ministry, cabinet, legislature, and courts of justice to appendages of the executive. The poorest citizen will refuse to abide by a decision of any intermediate and will take his case to the president personally. The president will see him. It may take months—but time does not matter. He will see him and set things right. That is, he will promise and give an order. If the order remains unexecuted or is lost in an inscrutable bureaucratic machine, it is not the president's fault but the fault of his bad advisors and associates. The president must say "yes" because he is a good man, a leader, all-powerful, in fact invincible. The people expect the president to be all-powerful. Otherwise, why should he be president? He must be the *caudillo*. He must be able to do everything he wants, or he will be unable to do anything at all. And there is no middle ground.

Under the circumstances, there are no immediate bases for either democracy or monarchy. It is interesting to recall that Bolívar recognized that the American milieu would erode any monarchy established there. He was equally skeptical, after much experience, of the former Spanish colonials' aptitude for democratic government. In his disillusion he predicted that America was ungovernable, a prophecy that proved itself to be true in many places and over a long time.

For one thing, government seems foreign and the law it enforces looks like an imposition. This was true in the colonial period and has been so ever since. In the colonial period government and law were foreign in the literal sense of the word. The governors were not only foreigners to the Indians, mestizos, Negroes, and mulattoes, but also to the *criollos*. Laws were made in Europe for a continent with entirely different problems and needs. In spite of their best intent, the officials of the Crown remained Europeans and Spaniards, and the law they wrote reflected their local allegiance and their local training. The natural consequence was that the law remained an empty gesture. The good intentions written into the law proved unenforceable. The Crown's officials, when faced with an unenforceable command, had a way out. They could say to the king that the law had been obeyed but not enforced, and that until the king's further pleasure was known, things would remain as they were. They could say to the king that they had acted to "save the king's conscience," for the king would not willingly do what was wrong. In this way—temporarily at least—the law and reality could go their separate ways under official license. The law was one thing; customary ways another.

All of this delicate juggling to preserve the king's conscience as well as his good purposes facilitated the growth on this side of the water of what has always been a good Spanish tradition: that the law is the preoccupation of government officials while the customary ways of the common folk continue as they always have—as if the law did not exist.

According to a well-attested story, no ship reached the Port of La Guaira in what is now Venezuela for a period of 11 years, and yet, miraculously, the cocoa of the country was regularly exported and the king's officials wore good English cloth. Something similar occurred in the United States during Prohibition when everyone on the block knew where the "speakeasy" was except the policeman on duty. When his official duty was over, he, too, of course knew where it was.

The export of American treasure and the import of European goods were to so large an extent in the hands of smugglers that effective rule in these matters lay beyond the reach of the law. Customary ways and legally prescribed rules existed side by side but unknown to each other, so to speak. This is but part of the story. In addition to the officials and the *criollos* who disregarded the law, there was the much larger Indian community which neither knew the law nor understood those who tried to enforce it. The Indian had his own ancient ways of determining right and wrong. The European colonial community was extraneous to the large mass of the population, which remained linguistically, and in most other ways, beyond the effective reach of the government. Where officials succeeded in enforcing the written precept, they did so as outsiders, as antagonists, as enemies.

The government and its agents and officials belonged to a different world. The state for which the government acted was an arbitrary entity beyond the ken of the Indians and in some sense beyond the acceptance of the Spanish colonists and their descendants. Even in Spain the Basques, Catalonians, Asturians, and others continued to live according to their own customs and traditions while the Spanish state and government were regarded as "foreign."

The Spanish tradition of a government apart from and strange to the people has survived in Latin America to this day. The "elected" official government is not part of the real substance of custom, common law, and local order. The representatives of the "government" collect taxes and arrest smugglers if they can. The government is not really chosen by the people and does not really represent them. This is especially true of areas where there are large Indian populations. These govern themselves to whatever extent allowed by the "official" government. The same may be said about large Negro communities. Government here, too, is foreign, and local regulation follows local custom and tradition. To a degree this is also true of regions where the local *caudillo* is the real ruler of the area and the "government" is a tolerated but suspected meddler in things that are beyond its "legitimate" jurisdiction. The government under these conditions clearly is not "our" government, and the law is not "our" law. The state and the government are impositions and the president and his officials either tyrants or impostors. The people in Yucatán, Cuzco, Cartegena, or Amazonas have never been converted to the idea that the government in Mexico City, Lima, Bogotá, or Rio de Janeiro is their government.

At the local level there is little instability, for on the whole the same people always govern because the effective loyalty and power is theirs regardless of who is the new president of the country or who are his agents. "Elected government" is important at the center; at the local level he who governs has always governed. In fact, at the local level the "election" is unnecessary, for everyone recognizes who the real "governor" is regardless of the election. If the president interferes by imposing his own "governor," the emissary finds the task beyond his powers because he can only do what the police or the army will do for him. He discovers for himself an old Napoleonic dictum: that the one thing you cannot do with bayonets is to sit on them. He may be the designated governor, but the real ruler of the district is the locally accepted leader whose power and influence have come to him "naturally."

What we are really saying is that the central government and the localities are two worlds apart; the lack of legitimacy and the absence of popularly endowed authority are a great deal more typical of the center than of the locality. The hope for political stability rests on the possibility of identifying the locality with the center, for that would be one way, perhaps the only way, of making the central government "legitimate." This can only be done in a democratic world through effective political parties, and no such parties are as yet in existence.

General Lázaro Cárdenas once remarked that "when all of the land belongs to the village then the government will rest on the village, but at present it depends upon the army." The reason why the government in Mexico rested upon the army was because no other institutionalized basis existed which was sufficient for the purpose. This statement can be generalized for all of Latin America. The only exceptions possibly are Chile, Costa Rica, and Uruguay. So far as the other Latin American countries are concerned—and this includes Brazil—the government's ability to survive to the end of the presidential term and its prospects for peaceful transference of power to the next administration are determined by the army's willingness to stand back of the president. Beyond the army there is no really effective underpinning for the government.

4. The American Example

In democratic countries such as Great Britain, the United States, or Switzerland, the government at the center comes into being in response to a consensus of the localities. If we take the United States as an example, the party in power is built from local cells, each having an effective role in its own parish and township and having long experience in local government. The local government, whether Democratic or Republican, is locally chosen in a free and competitive election. It serves a specific term, at the end of which it has to seek a new mandate on its record or be turned out. While in office it has local responsibilities in which no other agency of government is directly involved. The powers of the township vary from state to state, but in New York State the township collects the school tax, maintains the local roads which sometimes run hundreds of miles, has a zoning board, may have one or more sanitation, fire, lighting, and water districts, hires its own police, elects its own local justices of the peace, elects representatives to the county government, and performs many other services besides. The party in office fills most of these posts with neighbors who happen to belong to its local club. In the county and state nominating conventions, the local party cells are represented by delegates who help elect those who will represent the party at the national convention.

A local member nominated for a county office, such as sheriff, district attorney, or treasurer, is usually someone who has filled other posts in the township and has considerable experience in local affairs. His nomination to a higher office is a reward for local service sufficiently well done that his neighbors will vote for him. The same is true of the candidates who stand for election to the state legislature or to Congress. The local political clubs, or local political machines such as Tammany Hall, are independent political institutions which nominate and elect to township, county, state, and national posts those people who have found favor with voters at the local level or who have the loyalty and support of the local leaders. The Congress is not the creature of the President, nor is the Senate. The President cannot either prevent or insure the election of a member of Congress or of the Senate. Nor can the President interfere in the election of a state governor or depose him if he is in office.

For the purpose of carrying on government at the local level, each unit has its own taxing powers and collects and spends the taxes locally. Intervention by county, state, or national government is strictly limited by constitutional proviso and legislative enactment. The government at each higher level is chosen and maintained or defeated by the voters at the lower level. The government that comes to power is the chosen instrument of the localities. It is endowed with limited powers and for a limited period.

Moreover, the political party which nominates and elects candidates for office is an agency independent of the government. The President does not control his party. He may not even be its effective leader. This is also true at the state level. The governor does not control his state political party. In a sense, no one controls the political party of the state. The Hague machine in New Jersey could prosper in spite of federal disapproval, while the Westchester County Republican Club was able to survive a succession of Democratic administrations in Albany. In a pinch the President is dependent upon the local machine for the votes that will carry his program through Congress and he may have his program defeated by members of his own party who refuse to vote for bills he favors.

The party itself needs further characterization if this discussion is to help us understand the political differences between the United States and Latin America and to make clear what we mean when we say the governments in Latin America have no institutional basis because there is no effective political party system in Latin America.

The local Democratic or Republican club in any county or township may not have more than a small proportion of the total registered Democratic or Republican voters as members. Out of 1,000 voters the club may list only between 50 and 100 members, but they are likely to be active in the affairs of other organizations in the township, such as the American Legion, the Chamber of Commerce, the Elks, the Lions, local civic associations, all of which are centers of influence and power. These groups each represent a real interest. They each have their own defined objectives and defend, propagate, and promote a policy. They each have their own special definition of the world and of the good life, and they each communicate with many other organizations throughout the township, county, state, and nation. Their activities affect the lives of their neighbors and the activities of other groups. Each of these groups has its own leaders. Each group gives occasion for creative participation and a visible role to many of its members. Technically, these groups are not represented in the local political club. In fact, the club seems like only one more local group. But the political club is the organizer of local political power and nominates officials of government. It is the agency through which the objectives of the other organizations receive public sanction, support, and even legislative enactment. If these groups have no direct representation in the political club, they have in fact what Burke calls virtual representation through the participation of their own members. The political club is the center where the active public-spirited members of the community gather to argue over every issue that comes to the surface of public debate. If a question arises which is of interest to the Chamber of Commerce, the Volunteer Fire Department, or the Children's Society, someone who is a member of that organization will speak for it.

This process repeats itself in every township and in every city. It works its way through the party from the local to the national level and culminates in action in the state legislature or the national Congress.

This does not exhaust all of the influences that shape

public policy or that give direction to government. But when we say that the government has an institutionalized basis, we refer to the tens of thousands of political clubs under Republican or Democratic auspices, within which all of organized activity has virtual representation. These clubs lead to the nomination and election of one or another person to the House of Representatives, to the Senate or the Presidency. Clearly the President is not the creator of his own political party and clearly, too, his tenure in office does not depend upon the army.

5. The Political Dilemma in Latin America

None of this political complex exists in Latin America. There is no effective local self-government. The school, the roads, the police, the tax collector, and the agents of *formal* government are mostly in the hands of the central administration. The governors are appointed or are removed by the central administration. Federal intervention in the affairs of the states of Argentina and Brazil or in Mexico, where the central government has the authority to declare that a state has lost its constitutional powers, illustrates the central government's control over the state even in countries where there is a constitutionally established federal system. Most of the income from taxes is taken by the central government while the states, countries, and townships are left with a pittance.

I have seen a village that built its own school out of local materials with the voluntary labor of its own residents wait for months for the government to send the money to buy windows. A community needing a pipe or small gasoline engine to bring water to the village will send a delegation to the capital, where it will sit for months in the antechamber of the governor or the president. The state governments and the towns are forced to stand, hat in hand, asking for support from the president because the central government has absorbed most of the available income from taxes. All of this follows from the traditional principle of authoritarian and centralized rule.

In spite of the ancient and honorable tradition of the Spanish *cabildo*, there is really no way of organizing a national political party with strong roots in local government. Beyond the reach of the large urban center the hacienda, with its enclosed community of *acasillados* living inside the boundaries of a private estate, has no self-government. What government power there is resides in the owner, backed by whatever local tradition has grown up to define relations between the *hacendado* and his laborers. But the hacienda community, no matter how large, has no civic status. What authority there is on the plantation does not emanate from the people living on the place. These communities are comparable to our own "mill towns," organized around the Southern textile mills, where until recently the mill owner hired the policeman, the schoolteacher, and the preacher, and where the local factory "hands" had neither vote nor voice in the affairs of their own community.

In Latin America the hacienda, as we have seen, is a broadly inclusive institution, and in some areas most of the inhabited localities as well as a large part of the population are inside of these private estates. If the population on these haciendas happens to be Indian, there is usually the added barrier of language to make political communication most difficult.

The village outside the hacienda, if it is large enough, is generally controlled by the central government through one of its appointed agents, who may have the compulsory assistance of a given number of villagers. But, in Guatemala for instance, the real government, apart from taxes and purely legal matters, will be in the hands of a traditionally recognized authority completely alien to the central government. The central government may be ignorant of the existence of such an authority or contemptuous of its doings, considering them foolish Indian ways, but the effective authority in these Indian communities is with the traditional government and not with the agents sent down from the capital.

An interesting example of this can be seen today in Peru in the *barrajes* (shanty towns) which have sprung up all around Lima. Where the recent migrants in these communities are of Indian origin, a locally established democratic government—traditional in the Indian village—automatically comes into being. This government takes on the problems of the new community as best it can. All male members vote in the election of the community officers and frequent public assemblies are held to discuss the needs of the new community. But in Peru this government is legally nonexistent. The local communities there are officially governed by delegates from the center. Here is an interesting example in the capital of the country of two systems of administration, one legal and mestizo and centrally controlled, the other democratic, Indian, and legally nonexistent.

If Latin American governments had really been prepared to build a democratic society, here was (and still is, in many places) a good foundation to build on, based on custom and traditional folk law. But no political administration has ever contemplated such a possibility. The theory that citizenship is personal, that the state rests upon individuals, and the practice of organizing everything from above has made it practically impossible to incorporate into the legally constituted government the remnants of democratic practices and customs that still survive among Indian communities.

This leaves the mestizo or Negro communities, other than those on plantations. They are under the influence of a regional power system (see chapter iv) that exists independent of the central government. The central government meanwhile is represented by appointed officials except in those areas where there are elections for local office. Where there are elections, the central government manages to win, for it cannot permit the locality to escape from its control. Even in Mexico no governor of a state could be elected against the will of the president or against his known opposition. The governor of the state has to be a friend of the president. Furthermore, no governor could survive in office if he made it clear that he opposed the administration's policies or that he would not accept the decision about who the next president should be. Any governor who could defy the president on these matters would be stronger than the president and would end by driving the president from office. Even in Brazil where the tradition of federalism is stronger than in any other South American country, the president has often used his constitutional power to intervene in the state to displace elected governors by individuals loyal to himself.

In the large urban centers the situation is more complicated. In a number of places the most important local political power is in the hands of foreigners or, as in Trujillo in Peru, urban political life may be controlled by the large rural hacienda. Cities like São Paulo, Lima, and Santiago have increased in size so recently that effective political power still lies with the older oligarchy dominated by strong family allegiances—the same group to whom the central government belongs.

The oligarchy is one aspect of the extended family and reaches back into the regions. It certainly does not provide an effective basis for a political party system. As for the shopkeepers, small craftsmen, and workers, they have not really discovered their political interest or their power and are so dependent upon favors from the government that an independent party composed of these elements either serves only as political window dressing or stands in the wings waiting for the benefits that supposedly will be theirs in a future revolution. The time when they may constitute a truly independent political party is yet to come.

If the difficulties in the path of a possible political party system seem formidable enough, they are only part of a general social order which discourages private and group participation in public affairs. When one recalls the political impact of private organizations in a country like Great Britain, from the abolition of the slave trade to parliamentary reform, from the enactment of child labor legislation to the defeat of the Hoare-Laval agreement on Ethiopia, it seems incredible that such organizations have almost no role in public affairs in Latin America.

The president who comes to office in Latin America has none of the assurance and strength provided by a political party that has deep roots in the thousands of communities that form the nation. That is why he has to be the architect of his own power. He has no institutional backing except the army, and the army is unpredictable. It may support the president one day and turn him out of office the next. That is why he has to surround himself with people *"de absoluta confianza"* (of complete confidence).

This brings us back to Fidel Castro. During the days when he was in the Sierra Maestra with a handful of followers fighting to overthrow the Batista regime he had, on the report of those who knew him best, no ambitions other than the re-establishment of political freedom in Cuba. He wanted neither power nor office for himself. His task would be completed when the dictatorship had fallen and a new democratic government had taken office.

Both he and his friends should have known better. Latin Americans, as others, like to live in a make-believe world. They talked as if Cuba was a democracy with political parties and elections and as if the president was chosen by a majority of the people. The facts are quite different. The president was either himself a *caudillo* or was placed in office by one. The successor to Machado was Batista, and all of the succeeding governments were there by Batista's tolerance. The successor to Batista is Fidel Castro.

He does not have to be elected because his power would be just as unrestrained after an election as before one.

What once passed for political parties have disappeared because they were not parties but groups of office seekers in search of a leader who would, by controlling the presidency, authorize their misuse of public funds for private ends. Castro has no need of them and is trying to run an honest government. The announcement that he is organizing a political party—it makes no difference whether it is called Communist or anything else—is in his case insignificant because his followers expect him to govern, to make every decision, to lead them and to impose his will on any and every one who opposes him.[1] If he is making a social revolution, it is because he wants to make it. If he does not make one, it is because he does not want to make one. There was certainly no popular demand for the changes he is bringing to Cuba. The people who supported him in his struggle against Batista did not do so for this purpose, and had they foreseen what would happen to them, they would not have helped him come to power.

I am not arguing the merits of his program. That is beside the point in this discussion. What is at issue is that the power, the program, and the policy are personal. He is the executive, the legislature, and the judiciary. Every statement he makes is the law of the land. When he says that a man ought to be executed, he is executed. When he gets the idea of cutting the rents by 50 per cent, that is done. He governs by decree—that is, his wish is formalized into an official document and ordered to be

[1] There is, of course, a great dispute on this point. It remains to be proven that any party, Communist or not, can substitute for or take over from Castro. As long as he lives he will govern as a dictator. When he is gone there will be a revolution.

enforced. It is what his followers expect. They know who
their government is—Fidel Castro. They know where to
go for help, whom to call upon, in whose name to enforce
the law, and whom to blame if they do not like what is
happening. Beyond that, Fidel Castro claims a moral
sanction for his power. He destroyed the tyrant and is
now, as he has declared, bringing justice and liberty to
the people. As long as a sufficient number of his followers
believe that his intent is good and that his purpose is to
protect and help them, he will continue to be their hero,
a veritable prince returned to rule with divine power. He
is for them the king come to office again. *Yo el rey* has
reappeared.

His difficulties have arisen because his actions have become suspect. He has become suspicious and arbitrary.
When his remaining followers become fearful, as seems
to be the case with large numbers of Cubans, he will become increasingly tyrannical and will be plotted against
as Batista was. In fact this has already begun to happen.

He will find that he cannot resign his power, cannot
transfer it, and cannot abandon it. To be able to transfer
his power he would have had to come to office through a
political party which had strong deep roots in every community, a political party that chose him but might have
chosen someone else. The party would have brought him
to office temporarily and, when the time came, would pass
the office to another. But there is no such party, nor can it
be created overnight.

Fidel Castro would have made an important contribution to the democratic development of Cuba if in his announced intent to democratize Cuba he had decentralized
the government, reformed the tax structure so that most

of the income from taxes would go to the smallest political units, allowed the localities to elect their own officials without interfering and permitted them to spend their money as they thought best, and stood aside when there was mismanagement and corruption and allowed the courts to deal with matters that involved infractions of the law. But that kind of a program would have largely stripped him of his role as active leader. His followers would not have approved of it and the people themselves would in all probability have considered him weak because he permitted others to do what he should do—namely, govern absolutely.

That is the dilemma of Latin American politics and it reappears with every administration. Democracy requires local self-government and local power independent of the center and beyond its control. Centralization requires just the opposite: no local power and nothing beyond the reach of the chief executive. How the contemporary Latin American statesman who believes in democracy can work to increase local power and independence without at the same time undermining his own position is the unanswered question.

CHAPTER 9

THE UNITED STATES
AND LATIN AMERICA

1. *The Sins of the Fathers*

THE POLITICAL dilemma we have just described bedevils the United States' dealings with Latin America. Whatever our policy, we are caught up in the imbalance that for a century has moved from tyranny to revolution, from popular upheaval to dictatorship. Because Latin American governments are unstable, any action on our part is suspected of abetting or opposing this or that party, this or that individual. The presumption seems self-evident even if we are innocent of any such intent. Our mere presence is interference, and the inoffensive activities of our representatives have political overtones. The American Ambassador in Haiti, Ecuador, or Venezuela cannot give a luncheon or accept an invitation to dinner with any political figure, either in or out of government, without in fact strengthening or weakening this or that party or increasing the political prestige of this or that individual. Our mere presence is a stumbling block in the path of spontaneous political development. The outflow of American energy is so all-embracing that even Fidel Castro's strenuous efforts to free himself from the potency of the United States will prove a futile gesture. Not even Russia can save Cuba from American influence.

Many things fall into their place as soon as we recognize this simple fact. It is natural for our southern neighbors to be anti-American, to be jealous of our power, envious of our wealth, and to suffer from both frustration and inferiority at our mere presence. All of this is unfortunate but inevitable. So is the sensitivity and the indignation at every seeming injury, neglect, or outright rejection. The turning to communism by some intellectuals is an act of defiance. As a way out of the ever-present shadow which is the United States, it is like looking in another direction and believing that one can free oneself from reality by running away from it. So it was with fascism and Nazism. So it has been with any of the alternative prospects that promise somehow to shorten the reach of the United States, to cramp our tugging at their way of life, language, amusements, and their social and personal standards. One could detail this in a thousand ways from the cocktail to baseball, from the American movie to the Cadillac, from frozen orange juice to nail polish, from Coca-Cola to the office secretary, and from the American advertisement on television to the lilting jazz played by the orchestra in the "best" restaurants. The Mexicans have invented a word for it—*pochismo,* the substitute of the foreign, especially the American, for local traditional Mexican or Spanish usage, belief, or attitude.

The emotional outburst against foreign influence, against *pochismo,* is not only Mexican, Cuban, or Latin American. One needs only to turn to modern Ireland with its revival of Gaelic and its insistence upon inviolate sovereignty, which enabled it to keep Dublin lighted while darkened London was being destroyed by the blitz, to recognize that the Castro phenomenon is not entirely unique. And one can—if he accepts the emotional tug of nationalism—recognize that Castro in his attempt to Cubanize the Cuban people was impelled to expatriate the foreigner, drive out the English words in Cuban Spanish, eliminate the changed manners that came with the tourist, television, radio, and the automobile, destroy the newspapers filled by American columnists and American comic strips, expropriate the hotels, bars, electric companies, factories, stores, farms, cattle, and sugar owned by Americans, and cleanse Cuba of the sound, the laughter, the play of the American. The attempt is a species of insanity and bound to fail. But in a world fragmented by an increasing number of small nations filled with zeal for local purity and excellence, crying the slogans of anti-imperialism and anti-colonialism, that such an attempt should be made is not strange at all.

We should not be surprised that many of our neighbors to the south find it difficult to adjust themselves to the expanding influence of the United States. It seems impossible to make one's peace with the great power to the north except by accepting it and becoming 100 per cent American, more American than the Americans—or by turning to communism as an alternative. It is simpler, however, to continue in a state of resentment. It has the convenience of being ambivalent; it allows for flirtation with American ways without fully accepting Yankee ideas. The escape to communism is more difficult and less acceptable because, taken seriously, it requires a repudiation of the Catholic tradition, the ideal of democracy, and the concept of the rights of man. Escape by immersion in the American milieu is not unusual among the middle class and among some intellectuals. It is, however, a route strewn with thorns and often ends in disillusionment.

Americans will not ordinarily accept these converts as equals and in personal relations often treat them with the indifference and coldness self-satisfied people are capable of. I have sometimes wondered why American writers trying to account for the resentful feeling in Latin America toward the United States have failed to point to the most serious source of our difficulties—the treatment of Latin Americans as inferiors. The reason is perhaps simple and innocent. We are blind to our own ways. We are heirs to a tradition about colored people and it influences all of our attitudes, feelings, notions, habits, gestures, and verbal expressions about them. I can hear the protest of some readers. But in this world of ours it is necessary for us to face up to the fact that our treatment of the Negro is the single most serious obstacle to our role of leadership in a world of nations which are inhabited mostly by "people of color." I remember one day in the University of Caracas in Venezuela when, after delivering a lecture on American democracy, a perplexed young priest rose in the audience and asked: "In the light of what you have just told us, how do you explain the denial of justice to the Negro?" I might as well not have spoken.

Our national policy can be remedied. New laws can be written and new interpretations by the courts can in time reshape the public image and give the government the reputation of fighting against this evil rather than abetting it. Public policy can accomplish that much. But how do we reshape the attitude, feeling, gesture, tone, and manner of a people raised in the belief that colored people are inferior by nature and that the white European and especially the American are superior? This way of saying it simplifies the issue, for somehow it implies that this is something deliberate that can be changed by talk and instruction. Unfortunately, it has become an ingrained manner we all carry with us, even those of us who would teach others tolerance, forbearance, and politeness. This is the price we are paying for slavery—the sins of the fathers are being visited unto the fourth generation.

How can we treat Latin Americans, especially those partly Indian or Negro, as we treat our next-door neighbors? How do we keep all of our built-in mechanisms of resistance, defense, and repulsion from coming to the surface when faced with colored people, when it has always been natural, right, and proper to behave, talk, believe, act, and be just the way we are, better and superior? How can we be different from what we are and how long will it take us to be changed? Our difficulties with Latin America are not merely economic or political. They are moral. We treat the Latin Americans as lesser people. We cannot really help ourselves and we cannot conceal our feeling. Latin Americans sense it in every gesture and attitude, even when we are condescendingly egalitarian.

That is why the United States is resented and watched with an unhappy sense of inferiority. That is why, as mentioned previously, the fury broke against Mr. Nixon. The crowds in Caracas shouted: "Little Rock, Little Rock." Mr. Nixon was not spit upon because we paid low prices for coffee or because there was a decline in the petroleum market in the United States, but because he provided the occasion for a release of rankling indignation. He was the victim of our own shortcomings.

2. Our Dalliance with Dictators

One of our difficulties in the eyes of Latin Americans is that to them we have seemed to stand in the way of social and political change. It is tragic that the nation which first repudiated colonialism, and for generations stood as the beacon light for peoples in many parts of the world seeking to free themselves from political oppression, should, in Latin America, be looked upon as a friend of tyranny and a supporter of dictatorship. I actually overheard one Latin American saying to another: "Every time we overthrow a dictatorship we feel that we have won a victory against the United States." We slipped into this posture unwittingly. Our people simply failed to note the implications of the fact that the democracy which we take for granted has not really had a parallel development among our southern neighbors.

The democratic constitutions in Latin America do not reflect the realities of their economic, social, and political situation. In extreme cases like Santo Domingo under Trujillo and Cuba under Batista the constitutions were in the nature of a falsification. In other nations they are a hope, an ideal to be realized in the future. Latin America is caste-ridden, authoritarian, and in many areas has not changed perceptibly in 100 years. "The Great Transformation" that passed over Europe and the United States as a result of the introduction of the machine and incorporated the masses into the political process left Latin America by the roadside. There, governments are neither representative nor based on the consent of the people.

We have tended to accept, at least in formal parlance, the pretense for the reality. In diplomatic discourse the nations of Latin America were presumed to be democratic when in fact they were little changed from what they had been at the end of the colonial era. These are generalizations, but certainly in 1910 Latin America was little different from what it had been in 1810. The social and political modernization of Latin America really began with the Mexican Revolution of 1910 and now moves forward with increasing speed. But our assumption right along has been that we were dealing with democratic nations symbolized by representative constitutions. This false assumption led to our identification with the existing social and economic structure and placed us in the difficult position of supporting a "feudal" system against the expanding popular influences.

The democratic society we take for granted is just beginning to emerge in Latin America and we have not identified with it. Our government and private investors have, inevitably perhaps, associated with the groups being troubled, displaced, or destroyed by changes we cannot stop, control, or even guide. It is our misfortune to be identified with those who are endangered by the upheaval and to find ourselves opposing the reforms which would bring these nations closer to our own kind of democratic society. In some way this is the major obstacle in the path of our formal dealings with Latin America. We have in recent years supported their governments on the assumption that they were our democratic allies. They were our allies, true enough, but they were not always democratic. But because they were our allies, we were prepared to support them against the forces that stood for the democracy for which we are the spokesmen.

Our identification with the ruling families has made it difficult for us—until the Bogotá Conference in 1960 and the *Alliance for Progress* in 1961—to recognize the legitimacy of the popular pressure for change. Our investments in Latin America are tied to the present order and would in some cases be endangered by any broad program of social improvement. The dilemma is very real and difficult to resolve. In theory, and by our long religious and missionary tradition, we are committed to reform not only ourselves but, if possible, our neighbors. What is the Good Neighbor policy, or Wilson's preachment for honest elections and democratic governments, but an attempt to implement a sense of obligation that has its roots in religion? Roosevelt's Four Freedoms and Truman's Point Four Program are all part of the same preoccupation.

The perplexities are real, and simple generalizations are misleading and sometimes false. It is not our policy to support dictatorships. It would run counter to every American tradition. In practice, however, we have been the friends of dictators, dealing with them as a lesser evil, or as the result of a *de facto* situation which in effect left us little choice. We have found ourselves on the same side of the fence with the dictators also because they, like ourselves, were anti-communist.

3. Anti-Communism

This seemingly natural alliance between the democracy of the United States and the "strong" men of Latin America has proven a snare and a delusion. We drifted into the policy easily enough, but we misunderstood its meaning. We were opposed to communism while Trujillo, Pérez Jiménez, Batista, Rojas Pinilla, Perón, and the others were opposed to democracy. They were not worried about communism—Trujillo, Batista, and Perón flirted with the communists when it served their immediate interests. What they were really opposed to were democrats, the people who wanted regular and honest elections, free speech, a free press, the right of petition, the right of public assembly, freedom from arbitrary arrest, freedom from torture, exile, persecution, and the constant menace of sudden death at the hands of the dictator's henchmen. And we to our—what would be the right word?—bewilderment, confusion, perplexity, shame, found ourselves supporting governments that violated the principles upon which our own government rests, imposed every evil on their citizens, and did it in the name of the defense of the free world and opposition to communism.

There is a great lesson in all of this. We were caught up in a situation which we misread. We divided the world between democrats and communists, between the free and the totalitarian governments. But that proved too simple a classification. There were dictators who, like the totalitarians, suppressed all vestiges of democracy, but because they did it in the name of anti-communism and because they were, or seemed to be, anti-communists, we called them democrats and welcomed them into the camp of the free nations. Worse than that, we were guilty of helping the dictators persecute leaders of the democratic elements in Latin America because we allowed ourselves the delusion of identifying the enemies of the local tyrants as our enemies as well. For example, we very reluctantly gave Betancourt, the actual president of Venezuela, a passport and threatened to deport one of the best friends of the United States, Germán Arciniegas, because Trujillo and Rojas Pinilla called him a communist.

Our relations with Latin America and with other parts of the world have been damaged by our making anti-communism the central theme of our foreign policy. This gave us a forceful role in the world. It made it easy to rally individuals and nations to our banner. It simplified the task of identifying our enemies and separating the black sheep in our midst. American foreign policy could take on all of the characteristics of a great campaign, even of a moral crusade. That was all very good. Unfortunately, it suffered from a cardinal defect. The policy was a negative one. We were passionately against communism but not outspokenly for democracy. We welcomed as allies all those who enrolled under the same banner, even if they rejected everything else we stood for. We not only opposed communism but had the mistaken notion that all opponents of communism were democratic like ourselves.

Because this has been a period of rapid social change

our doctrinaire opposition to communism has tended to identify us with the supporters of the status quo. In Latin America every dictator proclaimed his anti-communism every time he took away the liberties of his people. In the name of defending the free world, he persecuted those who asked for constitutional guarantees. In Latin America, the identification of a fixed anti-communist ideology with tyranny became so clear that professional anti-communists came to be looked upon as agents of tyranny.

How bitter and painful this situation became was illustrated one day when half a dozen Venezuelan newspapermen were talking about the United States' policy toward Pérez Jiménez, their ex-dictator whom our officials had decorated. They had all been in prison and half of them had been tortured. When they talked about our friendliness toward Pérez Jiménez, it was with bitterness and suppressed anger. They spoke as if Pérez Jiménez had been decorated just because they had been imprisoned and physically abused. This kind of feeling generated gossip and rumor that spread quickly and widely among the people and provoked fear and indignation toward the United States. The combination of the resentment stirred by our self-confident superiority and the hostility that followed our "support" of the dictator goes a long way toward explaining the unhappy posture we have acquired in the eyes of the people of Latin America.

The justification of our negative position—being *against* communism but not actively *for* democracy—was often stated on the grounds of "non-intervention" which, in turn, is another negative attitude. This argument was often offered with tongue in cheek not only because, as we saw at the beginning of this chapter, our mere presence and our every gesture is an intervention, but because our active anti-communist policy was in many ways a source of intervention on behalf of the status quo, even if that was not our intent.

It has been easy for critics of the United States to describe these policies as evidence of hypocrisy, pretence, and deliberate choice. It has been easy to accuse the Department of State of supporting or, if you prefer, suffering dictators in the name of anti-communism because these "strong men" also favored American business. Nor would it be completely honest to argue that this element did not enter into the picture. Certainly, it would be unrealistic to suppose that American business was disinclined to offer a brighter view of the dictators because they favored American investments. Nor can we assume that State Department policy makers were completely uninfluenced by the favorable attitude taken by American businessmen toward, say, Batista or Pérez Jiménez.

Latin Americans believe that the United Fruit Company dictated the policy of the State Department during the Arbenz difficulties in Guatemala in the years 1951–4. However, it would be the grossest of libels to repeat uncritically this overly simple, if not malicious, explanation of our policy—either toward Guatemala or all of Latin America. If, indeed, this explanation were the whole truth, it would in one respect be fortunate, for it would be relatively easy to correct. But the difficulty is of another order.

Our commitment to non-intervention made it easy for American businessmen to urge friendly relations with the dictatorial governments. What was originally evolved as a doctrine to restrain the United States from intervening in the affairs of our neighbors became a justification for friendly tolerance if not acceptance of such dictators as Batista, Pérez Jiménez, and Rojas Pinilla. The policy of non-intervention made it easier for our representatives to remain on good terms with these tyrants, even though they knew of the horrors being committed by them. Our purely negative policy eased us into being friendly to the dictatorships whereas we should have been actively supporting the democracies as the only effective means of opposing communism. The only way of increasing the influence and viability of democracy is by encouraging it.

During the crucial years of our anti-communist campaign we should have taken a positive position on behalf of democracy. We should have repeatedly asserted our support of democratic ideals and governments through statements from the President and the Secretary of State, and by declarations of policy from the Congress. It should have been clear and known that democratic governments would be aided by government loans and diplomatic support, that banks and foundations would be encouraged to co-operate with these governments, that we would oppose, isolate, and discriminate against governments that were dictatorial. It should have been our policy to protect the democratic leaders who were driven from their homes by the dictators. Our ambassadors, members of Congress, and the State Department itself should have protested publicly when the government of Rojas Pinilla tried to burn down *El Tiempo,* the great liberal paper in Bogotá, or when the house of former President Alfonso López of Colombia was burned down. Active support of the democratic elements would have strengthened them and would have increased the influence and viability of the democratic process. Despite all of the shortcomings and difficulties of postulating general rules for policy makers in Latin America, it is always possible to distinguish a Trujillo in Santo Domingo from a Lleras Camargo in Colombia and to shape a policy in opposition to one and support of the other.

I recognize the complexities of carrying on the business of the nation in a divided world. But our failure in Latin America was due to a lack of a positive policy in support of democracy. Had we had such a policy, then Castro would not have played his present role. In Cuba there was a real difference between Prio Socarros and Batista. The first, in spite of all the corruption, had come to office by an election and would have, at the end of his term, left it by an election. Batista denied the electoral process by a military coup. Had we taken a stand then, our difficulties in Cuba would have been of a different order. We would not have been identified with tyranny nor accused of supporting the status quo. The actual impact of such a policy on the political fortunes of Batista would have been doubtful perhaps, but at least our own position would have been clear. We would have been recognized as the spokesmen for a democratic order and would not have been accused of being the main supporters of tyranny.

4. The Status Quo

The old order in Latin America belongs to another age and is, in some sense, of another world. It does not pertain to the twentieth century. It is certainly not something that can be deliberately prolonged by a nation like the United

States, where change and mobility are perhaps the most conspicuous elements in our culture. The status quo is anti-democratic and incompatible with our anti-communist campaign. Latin American society, which has seemed petrified these many centuries, has suddenly become explosive—among other reasons, because there has been a sudden increase in population. The old stratified social and economic society cannot make room for the increasing numbers who seek a means of livelihood. There is no built-in mechanism for change in this society, and its authoritarian bias makes social mobility well-nigh impossible. The restlessness and the pressure for change in Latin America is not primarily due to communist influence. If responsibility has to be assigned to outside influence, it is rather the outpouring of American energy that has made the old ways no longer tenable.

We stir up the conflagration by our mere presence, by our innate egalitarianism, by our back-slapping, good-fellow attitudes, by treating everyone we meet the same way, by having none of the attributes associated with a stratified social structure, by really not recognizing the difference between a "big" man and a "little" man. We also contribute to the pressure for change by our incredible emphasis on consumers' goods through every medium available to us. At the same time, we do our best to sit on the lid or help the present governments sit on the lid. Then, when the explosion occurs, we find ourselves completely surprised and we blame it all on the communists, who, I am certain, are glad to get the credit for being the "friends" of the people.

The present situation was graphically described by a French anthropologist when he took a good look at the hacienda system in Peru: "Not since the thirteenth century has anything like this existed in France or in Western Europe." Serfdom, in which people are sold with the land, is not only a Peruvian institution. In Ecuador, for instance, at least 400,000 Indians are attached to haciendas as *huasipongos* under a system which keeps them tied to the land. This is the type of reality which makes it easy for dictators and difficult for "democracies." And our problem is to help the democratic governments to make the transition between the thirteenth and twentieth centuries without too much convulsion.

Our sympathetic attitude toward Latin American dictators has made the prospects of peaceful change more difficult. We have contributed to the disillusionment with democracy of many of the younger generation. They have seen repeated efforts to use the "democratic" process to bring needed economic and social change frustrated by violence and dictatorship and have noted our complacent acceptance, if not our approval, of these dictators and their methods. Is it any wonder that many of them have come to the conclusion that the United States does not believe in democracy for Latin Americans, as if it were something they were not fit for? Is it any wonder that they have turned to violence and authoritarian leadership as the means, perhaps the only means, of breaking through to the twentieth century?

We would, I am certain, like to deny this accusation. We would like to say that if there is a modern generation of Jacobins in Latin America, they have learned their lessons from others, from the communists. But most of them are not communists. They have merely lost faith in the democratic process. They do not believe it works under the conditions of poverty, illiteracy, and social rigidity characteristic of their part of the world. We are in part, perhaps more than we will acknowledge—or even be accused of—responsible for turning many of this generation away from a belief in democratic ideals and methods. Our failure to denounce Batista for overthrowing an elected government in Cuba, our similar failure to take a stand in Venezuela, Peru, and Colombia, has weakened us in our battle against communism and brought us the reputation of promoting dictatorships in defense of the United Fruit Company. But more important, if we had taken a stand in support of democracy, we would have strengthened the belief in and the practice of democracy in Latin America. We would then have had some reason to expect that social and economic changes in these countries could take place with less violence and with more regard for democratic ways.

We cannot stop change. We are, in fact, more responsible for setting it in motion than anyone else, and we cannot help continuing to abet the agitation and making the "hunger" almost unbearable. For we cannot, as a culture and as individuals, cease being ourselves or change the influence we have. We will either help the Latin American governments work their way out of serfdom and poverty into the modern, essentially American, twentieth century or be forced to accept the alternative of convulsive revolutions in which we will be described as the evil-minded shylocks who stand in the way of "progress" and in the path of the legitimate aspirations of the common people.

This is clearly seen in our position toward Cuba. So far as most Latin Americans are concerned—I am not speaking about their governments, for they often speak with tongue in cheek—Castro and the anti-Batista revolution he made have their sympathy, and we cannot say an effective word about the matter because we tolerated and, until recently, supported Trujillo in Santo Domingo. After all, Trujillo's government was one of the worst in the modern world. Yet this government was one of our allies in defense of Western "democracy." Our case against Castro would be much more convincing if we had denounced Trujillo long ago. We finally did condemn him, but Latin Americans say that the only reason we agreed to do this was to set a precedent for an attack on Castro. It is hard to live by a double standard and expect to be honored.

The anti-communist campaign in Latin America has for the United States proven a poor investment. The Walter-McCarran Act, regulating the issuance of visas for visits to and passage through the United States, has made us more enemies in Latin America than almost any other single official policy, and it has made enemies of those who were naturally our friends. The State Department must have thousands of complaints in its files from American ambassadors and consular officers and from private citizens about the harm the enforcement of these provisions has done to the good name of the United States. But so rigid, so overcommitted, and so sensitive has our attitude been on the issue of communism that any folly which could be classed as anti-communist was likely to become what journalists like to call a "sacred cow," something that could not be critically mentioned. This is what has happened to the Walter-McCarran Act. One could add that political intimidation—the fear of being described as "soft on communism"—has kept many people who know how damaging these provisions are from criticizing them in public. I shall confine myself to two instances.

Once when I was delivering some lectures in Venezuela it suddenly dawned on me that the feeling of friendliness toward the United States and even toward me as an American had chilled to the freezing point. No one would talk about what had produced this marked drop in the atmosphere. After digging around among my friends, I came upon the explanation. It was very simple. A highly distinguished member of the small group of families who make up the intellectual and political elite, a well-known Catholic, a prolific writer who published innumerable columns in defense of the United States and was a former Secretary of Foreign Affairs, had been refused a transit visa by an American consular official. He was not going to the United States. He was on his way to France to attend some international conference and he merely wanted to change planes in the United States. But no. The young consular official was sorry. There would have to be an investigation. It was on record that years ago, when Venezuela recognized the U.S.S.R., the man was known to have attended a reception at the Russian Embassy. Yes, but didn't the consul know that the United States had urged the Venezuelan government to recognize Russia and didn't he know that the applicant was once Secretary of Foreign Affairs and a friend of the United States? Yes, he knew. But the law made refusal mandatory. There would have to be an investigation. Special instructions would have to be received. The thing could not be done in less than three months and there was no assurance, of course, that a transit visa would be available at the end of that time.

The former Secretary of Foreign Affairs walked out and slammed the door and became one of the bitterest enemies of the United States. He continued to write articles about the United States, but they were no longer friendly and favorable. He became one of our worst and most influential enemies. What happened to him affected all of his friends and relatives, and these included through intermarriage most of the important people in Caracas and most of our good friends. There were enough similar cases to justify the establishment of a special airline that goes from Mexico City to Canada without stopping in the United States, so that Latin Americans on their way to Europe no longer have to submit to the humiliating experience of trying to get a transit visa from us while on their way to Europe. When I once asked the editor of the leading literary journal in Latin America why he did not call me when he went through New York on his way to Europe, he replied: "I go to Europe via Canada. You think I would let myself be insulted for the sake of getting an American transit visa?" And we continue to wonder why we are unpopular in Latin America.

The other incident which occurred just recently and which was related in a general conversation by someone whose name I do not recall, but who was involved in the matter, is as follows. Through the good offices of the American Embassy five students who were elected by their fellows of the Polytecnica, in Mexico, as the most worthy (or those who were chosen as the best athletes, I am not clear about this) were to get a special trip to the

United States. The prospect of such an unusual adventure stirred great enthusiasm among the students and good feeling toward the United States. There were parades, meetings, elections, and speeches. Finally, the five lucky winners of the proposed trip to the United States were announced. The date was set, the bus in which they were going was hired. The students had prepared a special send-off to the lucky ones and the United States was the most beloved of all the nations among the students of the Polytecnica. Then at the very last moment the consular officer came up with the sad story that the most popular of the five students, the leader of the group and the most beloved in the school, as a child of 12 had been a member of a forbidden society. He could not under the law be given a visa to visit the United States.

It was perfectly clear to everyone involved that if it was announced that the leader of the chosen group would not be permitted to visit the United States, the other students would refuse to go. The students in the Polytecnica, and there are 30,000 of them, would believe that the school had been insulted. The incident would be pointed to as a sign of American duplicity and disregard of the good name of their school and of Mexico itself. It was perfectly clear that the enthusiasm of the students would turn to gall, anger, and emotional outbursts. The students would surely march on the Embassy, there would be riots, there might even be serious violence. The matter would be taken up by politicians and the press. What was meant to be a gesture of friendship would in all likelihood turn into a major public scandal embarrassing our good relations with Mexico. At the last moment, when the news could no longer be withheld because the students were ready to leave, someone came up with the question of whether this was not a case of mistaken identity, whether the child of 12 who was assumed to have belonged to a forbidden organization was not another child of similar name and age. Thus the situation was saved.

5. The Support of Democracy

It has sometimes seemed as if Congress was bent on undoing with its left hand the good it was trying to do with its right. If the notion of mistaken identity had not been brought up, the resulting ill will would have undone whatever good will might have followed an entire year of Point Four expenditures. Clearly, the Walter-McCarran provision has worked to make the conduct of our foreign relations more difficult and continues to destroy much of the good will and friendliness resulting from the aid programs for which Congress appropriates large sums of money.

Our relations with Latin America, if one is to call things by their right name, have been calamitous. If that is the wrong adjective, how do you describe the public abuse heaped upon the Vice President of the United States? Just how much lower can a great nation fall in the esteem of its neighbors and allies? I am aware of all the extenuating circumstances—the part played by the communists, etc. But these are not explanations. Those who argue this way are hiding from the facts and seeking to clear their own consciences by throwing the blame on others. If we are unpopular, let's accept the facts for what they are and seek to understand how it is possible that we, of all people

—we who have gone across the ocean twice to make the world "safe for democracy" and to establish the "four freedoms"—should end up this way.

We have arrived at this juncture in Latin America by pursuing a purely negative anti-communist policy, by accepting the dictators and tyrants as our allies, and by supporting them when, in the name of anti-communism, they harassed, imprisoned, and, in many cases, killed people who were trying to work for the simple democratic privileges we take for granted. There are many other things in the picture, but so far as the populace is concerned, we are identified with their oppressors.

The surest way for us to regain the good will of the people is to make it clear that we are for democracy. The President of the United States, the Congress, and the State Department ought to repeatedly announce the simple fact that we are for human rights, for human freedom, for social justice, and for democracy. We ought to say that we will support a leader like Lleras Camargo and oppose one like Trujillo—and do it.

Apart from the disastrous invasion of Cuba, this is what President Kennedy appears to be doing. The difficulties in the path of what seems a very simple policy are numerous, but it is always possible to recognize the difference between a government that is moving toward democracy and one that is going away from it. We ought to support the first in every way we can—through loans, credits, and technical aid. We ought to do our best to isolate the second diplomatically and economically and make it increasingly difficult for it to survive. If we are the leaders of the democratic world, then we must let the people know it. No one ought to be as puzzled as the political leader of one of the Latin American nations was when he asked: "What is American foreign policy?" The question is difficult to answer. But surely we ought to be at least able to say that we are against dictatorship in the Western Hemisphere. This was not clear during recent administrations.

There are, of course, many other reasons for our loss of face among our southern neighbors. One of them certainly is the failure of communications between us. Latin Americans continue to remember the "big stick" of Theodore Roosevelt and the many interventions in the Caribbean and Central America. They continue to picture the United States as a nation of big trusts controlling our government. They continue to describe us as a "capitalistic" nation where individualism is rampant, where there is no social conscience, where labor has no rights, and where "materialism" has crowded all humanistic and cultural influence off the stage. That a few of the more educated and sophisticated people know better does not really affect the general image of the United States, and communist propaganda has helped to blacken it even further. Unfortunately, Latin Americans have not sensed the profound social revolution that has taken place in the United States since the twenties. They have no understanding of our egalitarian society, or of the fact that we have developed a broad system of economic security and still retained our political freedom. They have not learned of the federal and state policies that seek to defend individuals against the inherent indifference of large organizations.

But the fault is not entirely theirs. In some sense our people have not learned to talk about the new society they have contrived for themselves. Our language has not caught up with our revolution. Both "radicals" and "conservatives" talk about the United States as if nothing had really happened, as if we were still living in the nineteenth century. It is, therefore, no wonder that when our leaders talk to Latin Americans, they seem to describe the United States in the language of Adam Smith and Ricardo. To the Latin Americans we are made to stand for an absolute individualism and a freely competitive system as if the United States had no social security, no unemployment insurance, no Securities and Exchange Commission, no bank insurance, no Farm Security Administration, no collective bargaining, and no powerful trade union movement.

If we project a false image of ourselves, the intellectuals among our southern neighbors do the same. What they want us to believe in is an idyllic world, a world of equal men dominated by a humanistic philosophical, literary, and artistic culture. The intellectuals are seemingly unaware of the hacienda system, of the great separation between the rich and the poor, of the inadequate system of taxation, of poverty, illiteracy, and the essential indifference and corruption of the governing cliques. Clearly both images are false and neither side really knows how to present itself as it really is.

It would not do to leave this matter here, for the failure of discourse between North and South America is not solely because each has a false image of the other. In some way we have missed the meaning of the passions that stir the present generation. In a very real sense we are removed from the issues and fail to appreciate how deeply people feel about such questions as nationalism and colonialism. People in many nations are striving for economic well-being, schooling for their children, sufficient food, adequate medical care, human dignity, and especially for national sovereignty and freedom from domination by outsiders. For us these issues are no longer real. Except for the argument over segregation, our preoccupations are of a different kind. We are concerned with the cold war, national security, productivity and employment, the crowding of the highways by automobiles, the conquest of space, overcrowding in our colleges and universities, agricultural surpluses, and the money we can contribute for the development of pre-industrial areas without placing too great a strain on the American dollar. The United States and the nonindustrial areas, including Latin America, live in separate universes, and the matters of most concern to one lie beyond the basic preoccupations of the other. It is not simply that we do not understand each other. The discourse is carried on at different levels and we do not in fact talk to each other. Problems of space exploration, ballistic missiles, issues of conflict between the United States and the Russians, or the degree of unemployment and dislocation that may result from automation are beyond the ken of the people in Haiti and Ecuador.

It is natural and easy to give a moral twist to the discussion of these different preoccupations in the United States and Latin America. It is easy to say that we or they are at fault. In fact, parts of this chapter sound just that way. We are at fault because we ought to know better. We should be capable of carrying on a national discourse on two levels—that of a highly organized industrial society and that of a simple agricultural one, striving for national independence and economic well-being. We should sense the passions and be responsive to the clamor of anti-imperialism and anti-colonialism. We should understand the striving for economic independence and industrialization. We should sympathize with efforts to protect and manifest a national culture.

The facts, however, are different. What seems most passionately believed and most insistently defended by them may appear exotic and irrelevant to us. The emotional tone surrounding discussions of such questions as industrialization, the export of raw materials, and foreign investments sounds unreal to us. As a nation we have long since decided the right or wrong of these matters and are baffled when they are still fought over.

Our industrial society, and the complex issues generated by it, have obscured the meaning of the excitement now evident among Latin American nations. We do not really understand and therefore do not sympathize with the emotional qualities their questions are endowed with. The issues posed frequently seem to lack reality. Our insensitivity (if that is the right word) places us at a great disadvantage. Their restlessness manifests itself not only in a demand for sovereignty and independence but for freedom, welfare, and education. The increase in communications has made these demands more exigent. Popular restlessness may express itself in riot and rebellion. The Castro revolution has figuratively poured oil on the flames.

The task we face in Latin America can be put in a single question. What can the United States do to help bridge the gap that lies between our $2,500 average annual income and the $200 average in Latin America? I am not sure that I know what these figures mean. But they are official findings of American government and United Nations agencies. Whatever they mean, the difference in income is so wide that, until it is narrowed, we cannot expect our aspirations, projects, or policies to have any meaning for the people of those countries. We are not really in the same boat despite all our preachments, despite the Organization of American States, and despite our mutual anti-communist campaigns. We cannot expect the poor in Haiti, the Indians in Peru, or the Roto in Chile to understand American policy or to associate with American ideals, either economic or political. The governments of Latin America may give lip service to our ideals or honestly try to identify with the United States, but the governing families are usually as far away from their own people as we are, and that merely complicates the problem.

I am not arguing that the change in economic well-being is the important issue. What I am saying is that the move from an average annual income of $200 toward one comparable to that in the United States would generate so many activities, interests, and conflicts, and so affect their view of the world, that the people would be in a better position to understand and share our outlook on life and our political ideals.

The Castro revolution and the *Alliance for Progress* are both efforts to answer the question: How can a whole continent in deep poverty abide in peace in this restless world of ours when it is confronted daily by evidence of affluence among its neighbors?

CHAPTER 10

CASTRO AND SOCIAL CHANGE

1. *The Consumers' Revolution*

CASTRO has attempted through political means to achieve an egalitarian society and a mass market, both of which Americans have been promoting as ideals while quite unaware of their political implications. Until the *Alliance for Progress* the United States was indifferent to the social and political consequences of the consumers' revolution we have spread across the face of the earth. Ours is a peculiarly ingratiating revolution—painless, pleasant, and irresistible. We stir people's appetites for all kinds of goods, and offer them for sale cheaply, on credit, on the installment plan, or on trial. The one thing we will not accept is a "no." What we have to offer has to be accepted because it is good for people. It increases their pleasures in life, adds to the joy of existence, makes men strong and women beautiful. It is easy to promote, and it is done privately and for a profit. It requires no conspiracy, no party line, and is effective. It is, in fact, altering the face of the globe and modifying people's habits, attitudes, tastes, and ambitions. The great change of our time is the consumers' revolution propelled by the United States.

An excellent example of this world-wide upheaval is the Model T turned out by Henry Ford. The automobile has been more revolutionary in its consequences than Marx, Lenin, and Stalin combined. It has changed men's relations to each other and to nature. In the United States alone the automobile has killed off over 30,000,000 horses, taken the drudgery out of farm labor and greatly increased the size of the farm unit, modified the ways of courtship by moving it from the front parlor to the back seat of the car, undermined the little country town, made suburbia possible, raised rubber to a resource essential for survival, and, among a thousand other things, made Nasser a world figure because oil has to be moved through the Suez Canal. This is but one example of the impact of the increasing flow of goods forming the consumers' revolution. The American standard of living, which is the model we present to the world, also includes the electric light, television, radio, refrigeration, air conditioning, frozen orange juice, electric typewriters, and canned pea soup. These are things the common folk cannot resist, just as they have not been able to resist American jazz. America's impact is unofficial, private, and personal, and the government has had a minimal part in it. The promotion of good business has been an innocent venture, not meant to have any political consequences. Political influence upon foreign nations is supposedly reserved for official policy. But this view has proved to be wrong. The real American presence comes from the personal transactions of private firms and individuals, Official policy makers are relatively unimportant. What private personal business transactions are about is deeply revolutionary. They are, in fact, the most significant thing going on in the present-day world, even more important than communist propaganda. American private transactions are promoting an egalitarian society everywhere. The driver of a Model T or a jeep has the same rights on the highway as the man who drives a Cadillac. A man killed in an automobile accident is indifferent to the make of car that was responsible. A "status" society cannot survive a culture saturated with mechanical gadgets.

Americans are unaware of their role as the gravediggers of class-ridden and stratified societies. They are merely selling toothpaste, fountain pens, and modern plumbing. In fact, however, they are undermining the stratified society characteristic of Latin America and of much of the rest of the world. But we have been unable to see this because in our culture the emphasis is upon productivity, efficiency, and growth, requiring order, law, regularity, and the honoring of contracts. Our associates in the non-industrial parts of the world are the leaders of the existing stratified and aristocratic societies we are doing our best to undermine. And we will continue to spread the consumers' revolution by all means at our disposal because we cannot help ourselves. That, indeed, is the major American business in the world.

The fact that it is incompatible with a stratified society

riveted into "classes" made up of the *señorito,* the favored child of fortune, and the *pelado,* who stands beyond the pale of fortune and is fit only to labor is a matter of indifference to us. We are politically unaware of the meaning of the American invasion of the rest of the world. If confronted with our disruptive influence, we would deny it. If the society is breaking down, blame it on the communists. After all, we are only providing the things people want and are willing to pay for.

What I have just characterized was and remains a peculiar blindness on the part of our political and business leaders. We still fail to recognize that the "American Way of Life," the American presence, is incompatible with a socially and politically stratified world. A mass market requires an egalitarian society based upon the mass. We have remained unaware that the changes we are pressing upon the world are, in effect, political and social.

This is where Fidel Castro's role becomes important. He has dramatized for the world that the political revolution comes first, social and economic improvement later. There is nothing new about this. The New Deal was a political revolution that preceded and reinforced the mass market and an egalitarian society.

Castro has posed the questions: How does Latin America move from an economy of poverty to one of well-being without a political revolution? How does it achieve adequate nourishment, shelter, clothing, schooling, and public health? On all of these counts the majority of the people are insufficiently provided for, and the difficulties are increasing in both town and country. The mass of people have, of course, always been poor not only in Latin

America but in most of the world. But while they have been poor they have not necessarily been undernourished or hungry. What has made the issue of poverty more worrisome is the sudden increase in population which is outpacing the increase in food production. Less food per capita is now produced than in 1938. According to the United Nations, per capita food production in 1954–5 was 94 per cent of the 1934–8 per capita average. In 1958 agricultural production increased 1.9 per cent while population grew by 2.6 per cent. Raúl Prebisch says that over-all food production increased 1.3 per cent in 1958 and by 0.3 per cent in 1959. Poverty is deepening, especially in the rural districts. When one looks at Haiti and north-eastern Brazil, for instance, the situation seems beyond immediate remedy, no matter how heroic the effort. The sum of the available natural resources and available human skills are just insufficient to deal adequately and quickly with the immediate situation. I do not exclude the possibility of social revolution, but in Haiti or northern Brazil such an event would merely make things worse. The Haitian situation has lasted over 150 years and has progressively deteriorated because an increasing population along with continued soil erosion have made it harder for the people to do as well today as they did 25, 50, or 100 years ago. Descriptions of northern Brazil today echo those made at the turn of the nineteenth century. Anyone who reads Daniel P. Koster's *Sketches and Travels in Brazil* will recognize that most recent newspaper articles only repeat what was described with equal vividness more than a century ago.

The poor in Latin America are poorer today also because they want more than their forefathers did. Not only are there more of them, but they have learned to expect more of life. They want more of the gadgets we advertise. Many of them have seen our movies, heard the radio, or seen pictures in newspapers and magazines (which they could not read). New roads, such as the very excellent ones in Peru, have opened the way to the great city, and large numbers of people have arrived in crowded buses or on foot. They have seen the wonders of the modern world and they want to participate in it. Hundreds of thousands of rural Brazilians, Venezuelans, Chileans, and Peruvians have come to the metropolitan centers and decided to stay—living in growing shanty towns without streets, light, water, schools, or medical aid. But the lights they see from the hillsides are too bright to abandon and the house they have put together out of sticks and tin cans is no worse or not much worse than the one they occupied in the place they came from, for it, too, was made out of simple materials, reeds or unbaked bricks, had a dirt floor, no window or chimney, no running water and no bed. The new site is overcrowded and there is no land to till, but the excitement of the city and its evening lights make the difference. The city seems to contain all the things the poor desire but have no way of getting. The city is the visible embodiment of the twentieth century while the place these people came from is back in the thirteenth. That is why they can never go back. Places like Guatemala City, Port-au-Prince, Caracas, or Santiago are of this world while most of the rest of the land belongs to a society which ceased to exist in Europe centuries ago. The city has all that is modern, not just the bright lights. It has schools, universities, libraries, newspapers, running water, sanitation, hospitals, doctors, stores, and theaters, and its inhabitants have money and dark clothes and they wear shoes. Away from the city, the mass of the people have few or none of these things. In the country and in the little towns most of the things that represent the modern world exist for no one—not just the poor. This is the great mark of Latin American culture—the city belongs to one world and the rest of the land to another. Anyone who wants to convince himself of this can do so by going a few miles out of any city in Latin America, from Mexico City to any little village in Hidalgo, from Quito to any hacienda where the *huasipongos* work the land, in Brazil from Rio to any grouping of houses on a fazenda, from Buenos Aires to an *estancia* worked by temporary tenants, and in Cuba from Havana to any sugar plantation with its workers in a typical *batey*. The contrast between the modern city and the hinterland contains the challenge Castro poses.

2. Castro's Revolution

Castro's political revolution against tyranny, base corruption, and governmental indifference to the many needs of the populace was legitimate and inevitable. What was not legitimate and necessary was the turning of a political revolution into a totalitarian dictatorship. Castro had ample resources at his disposal to deal with the basic needs of the land. Cuba was rich, not poor. It had a higher average income than any country in Latin America except Venezuela or Argentina. Contrasted with Haiti, it was rolling in wealth. Argentina and Cuba are the only countries in Latin America where the average caloric intake is greater than the minimum requirement. What Cuba needed was an honest government that would save the estimated $200,000,000 stolen each year by a corrupt bureaucracy. That amount put to building houses, hospitals, roads, and schools would quickly have changed the face of the land. What Cuba also needed was an effective tax system. It required greater investments in consumer industries. Cuba needed increased investment for agricultural diversification and rural settlements. The nationalist urge sweeping throughout Latin America undoubtedly required an increase in the Cuban share of the ownership of industrial and agricultural establishments. It stood badly in need of an honest interest in education and in the development of an effective university. Castro had all of the means at his disposal to carry forward such a program and, as a national hero, he had the backing of the people. And yet he threw it all away to become involved in a political morass from which there is now no visible way out.

Just why this profound tragedy has come to afflict the Cuban people and, in the end, Castro himself will always remain a matter of dispute. There are, however, certain visible things which can be listed. They may not explain everything that has happened, but no adequate explanation can leave them out.

There is first of all the nature of the political situation in Cuba itself. No country in the Western world has had a history of political corruption so universal and so corroding. Nothing touched by the government was untainted. Because the central government controlled all of the political activities in the land, corruption was correspondingly widespread and infected political life in all places.

The political parties were merely means for distributing what could be taken from the governmental till, from private business in need of government sanction or favor, and from protected vice—gambling, smuggling, and prostitution. There was in fact no responsible or honest political party in Cuba. The two presidents who preceded Batista's last coup were both civilian, "democratic," and possessed of an earlier gallant history of opposition to the tyranny of Machado, but their administrations were irresponsibly corrupt. Anyone trying to give Cuba an honest government would not have known where to turn, nor would he have had any confidence that the new "revolutionary" administration would be more trustworthy than the old "revolutionary" governments had been. This fact must be written down as one of the reasons for Castro's nonreliance upon the existing political parties. If honesty in government was an objective of the revolution, then it could not be achieved by falling back on the older political parties and probably not by the immediate formation of a new one. Honesty may not be the most important political asset, but in Cuba the people had been so frequently disillusioned on this score that parties and political leaders had fallen into almost total contempt. Governmental integrity had become a popular aspiration. This then is one reason why the government of Fidel Castro turned its back on traditional Cuban political practices.

But a more fundamental reason lies in the nature of the attitude toward the political leader. This, as has been shown, is not only Cuban, it is Latin American. The leader has all the power of government and no one else has any. When, on the early morning of January 1, 1959, dictator Fulgencio Batista abandoned the government and, ac-

companied by his closest henchmen, flew to the Dominican Republic seeking personal safety and asylum, he left
a political vacuum behind him. All of the power had belonged to Batista, and when he left there was no army, no
police, no judiciary, and no congress. There was nothing
to substitute for the government that had vanished like a
dream. There was only Castro, the new leader coming out
of the mountains, who suddenly found himself possessed
of all the authority formerly exercised by Batista. He was
now the army, the police, the judiciary, the congress, and
the electorate as well. All of the power of the state had
passed into his hands.

For an understanding of the revolutions in Latin
America past, present, and those to come, it would be well
for us to ponder the meaning of Castro's sudden rise to
power. Castro had no substantial army, no political party,
no support from the unions, no strong following among the
rural laborers and small landholders. He had no philosophy known to or understood by the masses. Almost to the
day that he found himself in possession of all the attributes of the state, he had in his following only a few
hundred young people, mainly students from middle-class
families. Not until Batista's disappearance could he count
on even a few thousand men. The government became his
by default. There was no other source of public power.
The land was empty of authority until it was assumed by
the leader of a small band of ill-armed and ill-trained
young men.

Personal power has conditioned Latin American history
since independence and is likely to be the catalytic element in the current ferment for social change. If the revo-

lutions that are predicted by so many in and out of Latin America occur, they will come embodied in a person, not in an ideology, party, program, or political movement. They will appear in the shape of a revolutionary *caudillo* who, like Castro, will take over from a Batista or a Somoza, a Trujillo or a Perón. Political structure is fragile. A few riots have toppled the government of Ecuador. In recent months, attempts against the governments of Argentina, Colombia, and Venezuela have been made by young army officers. A captain or even a lieutenant with a few men repeatedly captures a radio station or telephone exchange. Loyal government forces then surround or kill the malcontents and the uprising fails. But the mere belief that the government could be overthrown by such a venture—a belief shared by many—sheds light on the frailty of governments in many parts of Latin America.

They are caught in a political dilemma from which they have not been able to extricate themselves. The centralized authoritarian tradition requires a strong personal government. When that is absent, rebellions surge up at frequent intervals until one of the numerous uprisings succeeds and brings a *caudillo* into office once again, and the cycle repeats itself. The revolutions are personal— Madero, Carranza, Pancho Villa, Obregón in Mexico, Paz Estenssoro in Bolivia, Betancourt in Venezuela, Castro in Cuba. This record holds for those who have passed across the political stage in the last 50 years, whether they have been liberals or conservatives.

If any one thing is certain, the revolutions of the next 50 years will be more like those that preceded them than like changes that have occurred in the United States. Latin

America has had a rash of imitators of Mussolini and Hitler and will now have a succession of imitators of Castro. Fidelismo will, in all likelihood, become a banner for aspiring political demagogues who want to break through the crust of a static society and find a place for themselves. By its nature this static society does not allow for political change without violence and without being embodied in a leader. If the leader happens to be like Castro, not only a national hero but a demagogue who brooks no criticism, takes no advice, and is shrewd, callous, and power-hungry, then, like Castro, he will be free to make any kind of revolution he wants. It is as true for the future as it has been for the past. Castro can be driven out only by violence, as were Machado, Batista, and so many other leaders.

The decision to make this kind of revolution was Castro's personal choice. No one else could have made it at the time. He had all the power and there was no restriction on how he used it. He could establish his own system of justice and take such lives as seemed right and proper for him to take. He could confiscate private property for public use as he wished. Until he is driven from office by violence or taken from it by death, no one will stop him.

The taking of human life at will is in the older tradition. There is nothing new about it. But the confiscating of private property for public ends, placing it in the hands of a government bureaucracy—that is rather new. Traditionally revolutions were justified by slogans that had a liberal ring. The new ones will be acclaimed on grounds of Marxian theory and social justice but, like the older ones, they will be embodied in an individual.

The age-old tradition of personal leadership is so deeply

imbedded that it affects every policy, program, and ideology. *Personalismo* will prove one of the barriers in the way of the hopes held out for the *Alliance for Progress*.

3. A View of the United States

Another barrier is the Latin Americans' persistent misconceptions of the United States. For one thing, Latin Americans have neither known nor valued their North American neighbors. On the contrary, Latin American intellectuals have always stood humbly before European culture. When they thought of themselves, it was as Europeans. If there was an indigenous note in colonial painting, architecture, and writing, it went unappreciated or was taken as evidence of a lesser competence. This attitude persisted throughout the nineteenth century. Every fashion in politics or ideas was imitated. Romanticism, positivism, Marxism, fascism, and existentialism have all had their votaries, their following, and their influence.

When Latin Americans faced the United States they saw it through European eyes, and to the Europeans all of America was inferior, whether colonial or independent. Whenever a European—Spaniard, Frenchman, or Englishman—looked at America, North and South, he saw only uncouth barbarism or at best a poor image of himself. Latin Americans accepted the European judgment because they read European and not American books and because they were educated in Europe and not in the United States. North Americans also looked at Latin America through European eyes because for a long time they too were reared on European literature and went to

Europe for their "higher" education. North and South America saw each other as inferior because each in its own way identified with, and adopted, Europe's evaluation of the other America and sometimes of itself. This sense of inferiority has persisted among our southern neighbors in part because they are piqued at being left out of the mainstream of modern history. First they were dominated and enchanted by Europe and considered as something of a poor cousin. And now, quite suddenly, the United States, identified by Latin Americans as the cruder nation, has extended its arena and acts in the world as an equal to the great powers, at least in economic and military matters. Latin America feels left on the margin of world affairs. No wonder that the League of Nations, the United Nations, and other international conferences became so important. They offered a place in the sun for those who were left to live in obscurity. When a Latin American nation can be represented on the Security Council, when one of its delegates can be president of the United Nations Assembly, it has really come close to the center of world affairs. This aspiration for place, recognition, power, and influence is an honest desire held by all nations of the world. Our overwhelming power is resented because it casts a shadow over their aspiration for equality.

The hysterics of Cuban nationalism are just that. Cubans want to be independent of us spiritually—not just politically or economically. They want to carve a niche for themselves, a special place where they will not only feel secure but will shine forth to the world as a unique historic personality. That is why they are so bitter. That is why the memory of the Platt Amendment giving the United States the right to intervene in Cuba rankles so and is seemingly unforgettable. The desire to escape from our patronage and to stand out in the world as a distinctive even if little nation—like Holland, Denmark, Sweden, or Switzerland, for instance—is the inner drive. The little nations in Latin America want only to be themselves, not tied to American apron strings or led by the American hand. This is a matter about which we *will* hear much in the next generation or two. The changes forecast for the future whether violent or peaceful, whether by "revolution" or by democratic process, are part of the effort to achieve "independence"—the second liberation, as the Cubans say. And this inner passion is the greater because *this* independence cannot be won by violence. It has to be found, discovered, achieved, realized, grown into—whatever the word—so that the miracle of being at home among neighbors, without being burdened by a sense of inferiority or exalted by a feeling of superiority, comes about.

This is a matter which neither the Latin Americans nor the United States can do much about. Perhaps no one can consciously do anything about it. If we stopped feeling superior, the Latin Americans might stop feeling inferior, but that is not certain and no one can tell either of us how to begin feeling less uppish or more at ease.

The contrast between the two cultures in material possessions is so marked that there is a suspicion, if not a conviction, on the part of the Latin Americans that we want to keep what we have for ourselves and not let our southern neighbors catch up with us. When Latin Americans talk of imperialism, colonialism, and capitalist exploitation, they have in mind our growing wealth and their seemingly increasing poverty. As the gap grows wider, we are accused of deliberately making them poorer so that we can become richer. Instead of recognizing that these changes are the result of a higher rate of saving in an in dustrial nation and a higher rate of population growth in poor countries, that they are the consequence of the cumulative growth of a scientific technology which, by its nature, becomes increasingly diverse, specialized, and re-productive in new tools, skills, and insights, they see their inability to achieve our productive pace as proof of the exploitative nature of United States' relations with Latin America. They say: "The United States is the chief obstacle to Latin America's industrial development." As foolish as this idea may seem to those who have an average annual income of over $2,500, it is not so incongruous to our neighbors who may have to live on an annual income averaging $200 or less.

They accuse us of keeping progress away from them. In their desire to become modern, they know they must eventually reject a system which does not allow for the egalitarianism of an industrial society. But to their chagrin they find the United States supporting the status quo. Our businessmen and investors have inevitably tied their own commitments to the political world as it is. Latin Americans who accept the desirability of change are faced with the prospect of having to struggle not only against their own past but against the democratic world they hope to copy.

This is especially painful because Latin American intel-lectuals—more so than most in the Western world—are preoccupied with their own destiny and with their culture and its direction. This may be a heritage of the king's conscience. Just as the king was woefully aware of the mortal failings and earthly shortcomings that might keep him from glory and from heaven, so Latin American intellectuals worry about the destiny of their continent and their culture. Where they are going and whether they will achieve glory and grandeur, something unforgettable to all of mankind, is a continuing preoccupation of the most serious writers and thinkers. The fact that other peoples have managed to develop great cultures without this almost morbid awareness of self and destiny is beside the point. Their Spanish heritage provides a sense of moral purpose not only for the individual but for the whole continent. Don Quixote is still very much alive. We in the United States, who have for so long taken our destiny for granted, who allow tomorrow to worry about the next day while we live and work in the present, find ourselves portrayed by Latin Americans, who are preoccupied with the future and the ultimate, as short-sighted, materialistic, and spiritually drab. In their view of the matter, our chief concern has been immediate enrichment. As such, we could only be morally obtuse.

It is this view of the United States that helps explain certain facets of the Cuban revolution. Castro is anti-American and denounces us in hysterical terms because he not only wants to be free from American influence but because he has repudiated our claim to superiority. He asserts that the Cuban spirit is higher and richer. To be free, Cuba must, in Castro's view, repudiate not only its dependence upon the economy of the United States but totally free itself of American influence. It must be Cuban and only Cuban. This hysteria is present, real, and self-defeating. But it is part of the mood, and Latin America's early approval of Castro is largely explained by his repudiation of the United States' claim to greater virtue. In this he was expressing their deepest feelings.

4. Cuba and Mexico

Castro's difficulties at home and abroad began when he decided to make an agrarian revolution in a country that had no agrarian problem and was preponderantly urban and commercial and tied to the international price system. He mistakenly identified social reform with agrarian revolution and obviously took his model from Mexico.

But Cuba is not like Mexico. To begin with, Mexico is an Indian country. In 1910, when the Mexican revolution began, at least 50 per cent of the people were Indian, spoke little or no Spanish, followed the customs of their forefathers, lived in little isolated villages without any idea of the nation, and retained traditional attitudes and ways that made the phrase *Patria chica,* the little nation, a meaningful expression of localism and regionalism. Nothing like this can be said about Cuba. The few primitive Indians disappeared in the early years after the discovery, to be replaced by Negroes coming from Africa. The mass of the people are part African rather than Indian. On at least two occasions in the nineteenth century—in 1817 and 1843—the African people outnumbered the European. Slavery lasted until 1890. By Cuban definition 12.7 per cent of the population is colored at present. In Cuba the Negro played the part played by the Indian in Mexico. The Indian was sad, serious, quiet, bound by traditional mores, immersed in the affairs of his village and family, devoutly religious, mystical, and indifferent to the ways of the white man. The Negro in Cuba, on the other hand, filled the land with the drums and the dance, conserved few traditions of his own, had no attachment to the land, and was not identified with any village, community, place, or region that was his own. He was confined mainly within the ambit of his master's domain, and never, even after independence from Spain, became absorbed within the discipline of a community that ruled its own members by a customary law which could be broken only at one's own peril, which expected each member to take his share of the burden of local affairs, as did the Mexican rural community. One must never forget that the Indian community in Mexico exacted a kind of civic responsibility from each member from childhood to old age and lived by a kind of internal self-government which preserved the community and marked it as a collective body (even if not a legal one). When the revolution came, the village proved a very effective source of power. But nothing like this ever existed in Cuba. There are, in fact, no villages in Cuba. The *batey* (the premises of a sugar mill), the typical Cuban rural grouping, is located within the plantation, is subservient to the owner, and was originally composed of slaves. In recent times it has been made up of workers who had only an incidental attachment to the place of their abode. Whereas in Mexico even the hacienda community often consisted of people whose ancestors had lived in the place and who preserved around the church the forms of an organized religious community, the Cuban country folk have never had the traditions of an established rural community.

In 1910 Mexico was a rural country. Out of some 15,000,-
000 people which the census attributed to the nation, only
about 5 per cent lived in urban centers. The Mexican revolution, therefore, began in a nation where most of the
people were close to the soil, made their living from tilling
the land, and knew nothing of the ways of the city. This
was also the case in Bolivia in 1952. The same can be said
of Russia in 1917 and of China when it began its social
revolution. In Cuba, however, the urban population in
1953 was 57 per cent and now is at least 60 per cent of
the total. (In 1953, 63 per cent of Cuba's dwellings were in
urban areas.) Havana alone contains about 20 per cent of
all of the Cuban people.

It is important that the reader note that what we call
social revolutions have all occurred in agricultural countries where the mass of the people lived on what they
themselves raised from the soil. In such a society, a revolution is a simple thing. First, you cut off the head of the
hacendado, then you divide the wheat, corn, and barley
stored in the barn and the *hacendado*'s cows, horses,
sheep, and chickens. Similarly the plows, digging sticks,
and other tools are distributed. The land is taken by the
peasants and the revolution is over. What really happens
is that the stored consumer goods are divided up among
the surrounding peasants, and the limited producers'
goods, in the form of seed, animals, tools, and the land
itself, fall into the hands of those who have used the tools
and animals and worked the land. They have the knowledge, skill, and experience needed for their continuing
use. In that sense the real income of the rural population
increases or is expected to increase at the expense of those
who have been expropriated, driven out, or killed. Simul-

taneously, the income of the urban population declines. This is what happened in Mexico, in Russia, in Bolivia, and, one would assume, in China. In Russia, the communists went out into the country and by force of arms collected food for the urban proletariat. That was possible in Russia because the urban population was relatively small.

But in Cuba the urban population is no more capable of feeding itself than New York, London, or Berlin. It has to be fed from the outside. Plutarco Elías Calles could, as late as 1930, say of Mexico City: *"No cuenta"*—it does not matter. Castro cannot say that about Havana. Like all large urban centers it is a complex of commercial and industrial activities. Its people make their living by earning money and then purchasing their food. If the food were not available, they would starve in spite of their money. But in Cuba it is not possible to bring in enough food from the rural districts. Cuba does not produce all of the food it consumes; about a third of its imports have been food items. This is the basic distinction between the Cuban revolution and the Mexican. Cuba is a commercial and industrial economy whereas Mexico was a subsistence economy. Mexico had no national market, most of the food was locally produced and locally consumed, and what was exchanged was bartered in parochial markets. Cuba, on the other hand, has long lived on what it could import from the outside. Its entire population lives in a monetary economy, whereas the vast majority of the people in Mexico in 1910 lived outside the money market. But in a monetary economy income is not increased by expropriations, revolutionary zeal, or denunciations of Yankee imperialism.

This really brings us to the crux of Castro's difficulty. An urban monetary, commercial, and industrial economy cannot be treated like one that depends upon subsistence agriculture.

The only way to increase the income of the mass of the people in a monetary and industrial society is to increase production at home or to increase the amount that can be purchased from outside. It is as simple as that. Only by having more goods available can the people find more to eat and wear. Increased production is something that cannot be obtained by expropriation or by revolutionary slogans. If most of the population is urban and if the entire population lives on a money economy, the Mexican model for revolution is a bad one. It can only lead to a lower standard of living for the entire·population, not just for those living in the cities.

This is true despite the Marxian doctrine of the class struggle in urban and industrial areas and the concept of a proletarian uprising against the capitalists. The successful uprisings, in fact, have occurred in countries where there were relatively few proletarians in the Marxian sense and few capitalists. There is no single instance of an attempt by an industrial population to tear the society apart and distribute the goods they could lay their hands on. Intuitively the populace knows that it would gain nothing by dividing the subway and allowing the workers to carry a piece of rail home. If the Marxian concept of the class struggle has reality, it is to be found in a stratified agricultural society where the distance between the *hacendado* and the peon cannot be bridged, where there is no middle class, and where there is no built-in mechanism for social and economic change. In those societies social revolutions have occurred and may well occur again. But in no industrial and monetary society has all of Marxian theory produced a single truly proletarian uprising. A revolutionary uprising is simply not a viable means for social change in a monetary, commercial, and industrial society.

This view of the nature of revolution places Castro in a most difficult position. Having defined the Cuban problem as primarily an agrarian one, he initiated a series of policies which did not meet the needs of the Cuban economy and which could only damage Cuba and its people.

It is, however, understandable why Castro took this direction. If he was going to make a revolution, then Mexico, Russia, and China were living examples he could study. The fact that Cuba was not like these countries was not easily visible to one brought up on the idea of the class struggle. Given the Marxist background of so much of the political thinking and writing in Latin America, and given the Mexican example, it was natural for Castro, when possessed of the power of government and filled with revolutionary zeal, to turn to land reform as the great panacea, as the basis for all else that the revolution might hope to do in the future. Unfortunately for Castro and for Cuba, he did not realize the significance of the fact that the urban population of Cuba greatly outnumbers the rural and that all of the people are enmeshed in a monetary economy dependent primarily on the export of sugar at a world market price over which Cuba has no control.

Certainly Cuba faced serious problems in education, health, and housing. It suffered from large-scale rural and urban poverty and unemployment. But Cuba did not have an agrarian problem.

For one thing, the mass of the people had no tradition of

farming. There were no thousands of villagers (as there had been in Mexico) who remembered that the surrounding lands now occupied by the *hacendado* had once upon a time belonged to their forefathers and had been taken by force. There was no tradition of peasant uprisings. There was, in fact, no demand for land distribution. Castro was no Emiliano Zapata fighting the battle of the villages in Morelos. The notion of agrarian reform was something Castro had learned abroad. It did not emanate from the people. It never really occurred to them because Cuban agriculture, for many years past, had been geared to the production of sugar, tobacco, and coffee for export. These crops (especially sugar) were grown on large estates, mainly with migrant labor. The small self-sufficient farmers who could benefit from land distribution were few.

Furthermore, a sugar plantation cannot be broken up without destroying its efficiency. To operate at all, the work of the plantation must be so organized that the planting and the cutting of the cane can be scheduled to provide a regular flow of new-cut cane as it ripens during the four or five months of the grinding season.

The central office must have unified control over the labor force and the loading and the maintenance of the animals, wagons, trucks, or railroad cars that are part of the operation. It must also be able to deal with plant disease and the danger of fire. Once set in motion, the *ingenio,* the sugar factory, has to keep going until the *zafra,* the sugar harvest, has come to an end.

What we have described is a factory in the field and not a farm. If agrarian reform had not been an obsession based upon Mexican experience, it would have occurred to no one that the way to deal with Cuban difficulties was by dividing the large sugar plantations.

That the sugar plantations cannot be broken up must have become clear to Castro and his advisors early in their program. For, instead of breaking up the estates, they have been taken over by the government and entrusted to an agency popularly known as INRA (*Instituto Nacional de Reforma Agraria*). The workers on the plantation are organized into "co-operatives," but effective control is in the hands of the government. INRA has replaced the former owners and instead of 161 separate plantations under separate management there is now just one employer and one manager. The "co-operatives" are merely the tools through which INRA operates the industry. INRA gives the orders, pays the wages, often in scrip which can only be exchanged in the stores, it maintains and finally purchases the crop from itself at the price it sets. What has really happened is that there is now only one employer, one supplier, and one purchaser. For the sugar-cane cutter these changes have been dramatic and of dubious value. Before the revolution, the worker could complain to his employer, could take his grievance to his union, and could go on strike and appeal to the government for help against the owner—something that happened many times. The owner or his representative was at hand and was amenable to union persuasion or pressure and to the threat of the government. Now, however, the "owner" is far away in a government office guarded by militiamen armed with machine guns, and the trade unions have been stripped of their power and are under the thumb of this same owner. Most dramatic of all, the "boss" and the policeman are now one and the same person. The worker has no recourse and no one to turn to. What started out to be a liberating social movement in the guise of agrarian reform has turned into a monopoly of all economic, social, and political power, immune to either persuasion or pressure. The government has become omnipotent and controls the greater part of the agricultural plant.

INRA's control over agriculture has been increasing. The *Granjas del Pueblo,* the newly organized "people's" farms, now contain more acres than those in sugar and are operated directly by the state under a system of wage-paid labor. These have replaced many small farms, including those growing tobacco.

If one remembers that this adventure in centralization embraces the industries that provide the major source of foreign exchange and a large part of the national income, it follows that control of the rest of the economy was inevitable. But the control of well-nigh all the country's economic and social activities by a single bureaucratic agency automatically impels the government to depend upon force as its major instrument for implementing its program, and the policeman in Cuba now rules every facet of human life. With no intermediary power to stand between the individual and the government, the police inevitably become the sole disciplinary agency.

It must now be evident that an industry upon which the life of the nation depends is something more than a mere land problem. Where the elemental things that make up the people's standard of life have to be imported, the resource which makes these imports possible can be meddled with only at the risk of jeopardizing the well-being of the people themselves.

These changes in Cuba were wrought in the name of a future egalitarian society and have been imposed upon a people proud of their sense of freedom and their delight in song and dance. To force the Cuban people to conform to some preconceived design and to convert them to a severe puritanical outlook on life will require painful effort and will fail in the end.

In contrast to what is going on in Cuba, the Mexican revolution had more modest ends. The changes that have followed in the wake of the Mexican upheaval have been the by-products of a popular movement whose leaders came from the bottom and had no fixed design to impose on the nation. The Mexican revolution did not concentrate all power in a single man's hands nor did it make one man's voice the only one that could be heard in the land.

5. The Alliance for Progress

Castro has dramatized the political basis of social and economic renovation. The *Alliance for Progress* is our belated recognition that political change precedes social reform. Much social and economic change in the world takes place informally and unconsciously, without deliberate decision or formal policy. But when men set out to change the institutions about them they have to base their policy on some sort of consensus, some moral justification and some political sanction. We have been engaged for many years in promoting an egalitarian society and a mass market. We have come to the point of recognizing that the industrialism we promote cannot coexist with a stratified social and economic structure. The political system which maintains such stratification must yield to demands for greater vertical mobility, for a more equitable distribution of income, and for easier access to schooling. We now recognize that the very poor, the excluded, those who were sold with the land, and those for whose children there was no access to the modern world, can no longer be kept in their traditional place without provoking a violent upheaval or frustrating and slowing the consumers' revolution we have been promoting. What we are really saying is that since the world we represent is no longer compatible with the present state in Latin America, we will help contrive the necessary political changes to allow for a peaceful dissolution of the stratified society.

For the first time in our history we are setting out to promote social and economic reforms in foreign countries as a matter of public policy. We are telling our neighbors to change their land system, their tax structure, their education, and their political organization as a condition of our helping them to establish an egalitarian society more quickly. We are really telling the leaders of Latin America —the aristocratic families who have ruled the land for 400 years—to surrender not only the basis of their social status and economic well-being but the source of their political power as well. We are telling them to do this as a condition of receiving our aid in industrialization which, if successful, will promote an egalitarian society and a mass market and destroy the basis upon which the present political system rests. We have, in fact, taken our stand on behalf of social revolution. We are probably doing this unconsciously without understanding the full implications of land reform, tax reform, universal education, etc. The present system in Latin America rests on the large plantation, on inequality in taxation, illiteracy, an impossible gap between the *señorito* and the *pelado*, and on the idea of a natural aristocracy surrounded by followers and servants. The leadership of Latin America believes in paternalism, charity, and the idea of the *compadre* (godfather), but not in equality, not even as a price for industrialism. Those who do believe in equality, social reform, and social revolution are a small number of intellectuals, students led by Marxists, and a few labor leaders in the grip of communist ideology who—with Sputnik and Castro before them—believe that everything is made possible by revolution. One need only take a careful look at the present political complexities of Colombia, Argentina, Ecuador, and Guatemala to recognize how difficult it would be to predict the consequences of any political program brought in from the outside.

What we have committed ourselves to is the promotion of social reform by peaceful means on the assumption that the present governments will change political and social institutions sufficiently to enable them to move ahead toward what we understand by democracy. But one would have to be an optimist to believe that such a policy can be successfully initiated and carried through by the present governments. Any such program will be resisted by the aristocracy because, in effect, it amounts to self-liquidation. A successful agrarian reform in the highlands of Peru would destroy the political power of the mestizos in the towns, who own the lands that the Indians on the plantations and the villages work. This is what happened in Bolivia after the revolution of 1952. The Indians who acquired the lands also acquired political power. To believe that the present or any similar government in Lima would or could carry through such a plan is to forget the history of Peru. Something like this can be said about nearly every country in Latin America.

Without profound social and political reform, the egalitarian democracy we stand for is impossible. It is also unlikely that the governments of Latin America can carry forward the necessary changes. In the face of this, there are really only two possibilities. The pragmatic one, the one we ought to pursue, is to promote industrialization as best we can and let the changes occur as they may. They will be intermittently peaceful and violent, but our role will remain that of supporting the development of industrial growth, housing, education, etc., as we can, without commitment to a particular political program and without asking for specific change in governmental policy. This would enable us to define our responsibility for social change as limited to helping governments meet their problems, even if they come to power by violence. Or we can, as we apparently are doing, commit ourselves to promoting social changes which would in effect destroy the present basis of government in Latin America. We are not deliberately bent on overthrowing the age-old ruling class in the southern part of this hemisphere, but that is what agrarian reform, tax reform, and the other items of our policy really come to.

It will not be surprising if these proposals of ours do result in a whole series of social revolutions where the slogans will be derived from statements by American political leaders. The revolutions may well be made in our name rather than in that of Russia, but we will not be able to control them. They will be made by leaders who will find their justification in the *Alliance for Progress*. This is a bit of prophecy that may not come true. We may simply foment the revolutions and have the communists take the credit for them and control them, for we are unlikely to support any government that comes to office by violence, that kills or exiles our friends. Yet this is just what a social revolution means, and the changes we are proposing as a condition of our help may well produce these results.

The gap between the rich and the poor in Latin America is so wide that it cannot be bridged in a hurry, except by violence, and perhaps not then. To speak of this as a ten-year program is to speak of ten years of convulsion, or of a magic universe where miracles can be performed. Ultimately the gap can be closed by changes stimulated by industrial developments. This would be, as we said, mainly a peaceful process but also sporadically violent. It would, so to speak, ease the backward parts of Latin America into the present in gradual stages, as developing resources permitted. To attempt to hasten this process by our pushing reform as a condition of help toward development will either bring military dictatorship in its wake as a way to avoid social convulsions or produce violent outbreaks without necessarily accelerating the desired social changes. Anyone who believes that an egalitarian democracy can be developed in ten years in Guatemala is due for an unhappy awakening. Not all the resources at our disposal if they were all dedicated to Guatemala could produce this result in that short time. It is like asking how much money it would take to erase racial feelings in Mississippi in ten years. The remedy might in the end prove worse than the disease. Our political responsibility for egalitarian revolution could be satisfied if we accepted social changes as they occurred and did our best to help the governments deal with the difficulties that follow in the path of industrializing a stratified society. But up to now we have refused to admit that rebellions or demands for change had any legitimacy. There is one exception to this rule, and that is Bolivia, where we have accepted the revolutionary government and worked with it.

This is not meant to sound like a criticism of the *Alliance for Progress*. It is meant to question the emphasis on "conditions" to be met before aid is given. With or without our aid, there are likely to be many upheavals in Latin America in the next 25 years. We have to learn to accept these revolutions. Their number will decline as the countries become industrialized. In the meantime, we cannot work miracles and the "Marshall Plan" will prove more difficult to apply in Latin America than it was in Europe. It will be some time before Latin America can take a "Marshall Plan" in its stride. Could a Marshall Plan have been applied in Europe during the years of the French Revolution? It is no exaggeration to say that the greater part of Latin America is closer to the Europe of the French Revolution, before the industrial revolution had spread to the Continent, than it is to the Europe after the Second World War when the Marshall Plan was developed.

6. A Policy Proposal

The real question faced by the United States and other industrial nations is how to allow for the seemingly necessary revolutions among pre-industrial countries without unduly interrupting their development—that is, without interrupting the flow of foreign investments they require if they are to industrialize at more than a snail's pace. Every revolution, among other things, confiscates foreign property, perhaps merely to prove its zeal and patriotism. This is due partly to nationalist self-identification and partly to Marxist belief in the essentially evil nature of "capitalism and imperialism." The issue is grave enough to require some corrective measures in the interest of the pre-industrial areas themselves, for confiscation not only slows down further investment and stimulates a flight of capital from areas where it is most needed but also disrupts and sometimes destroys the industrial plants already in existence and postpones the possibilities for increasing the standard of living of the people in whose name the revolution is made. This issue goes to the heart of the relations between the industrial and nonindustrial nations whose aspirations for liberation and economic independence both seem involved in the right to confiscate foreign property. The fact that confiscation either postpones or retards the economic expansion a growing population requires is lost in the revolutionary excitement. Political measures need to be developed to sustain the objectives of social reform and protect the foreign investor at the same time.

The number of industrial nations in the world are limited—the United States, England, France, Germany, Japan, and a few others. These nations supply the capital for both short- and long-term investments. Every railroad, factory, mine, or power station in the wide world has come from the resources made available by the citizens or governments of this limited number of nations (joined by Russia and its satellites in the last few years). All of the rest of the nations of the world secure their international exchange by the export of raw materials to these same few nations. The underdeveloped nations—whether exporting coffee, cocoa, sugar, bananas, cotton, tobacco, meat, wheat, copper, nitrates, or silver—find their chief available markets in the industrially developed nations. This should make it possible for the industrial nations, individually or collectively, to develop measures which would protect their own investments and prevent the disruption of the industrial growth of a nation caught up in a revolution. The issue can be illustrated by Cuba.

In the light of what happened in Cuba all of our investments in Latin America are in jeopardy. The *Alliance for Progress* could not survive another Cuba, and Latin American industrial development would be seriously retarded. However, confiscation feeds the political excitement new governments need and satisfies latent nationalism and the desire to be complete master in their own house. Following the Cuban example, it has become a fashionable way for that kind of government to behave. It is easy and all it requires is a decree. It is dirt cheap, for it costs nothing at all, and it seems to transfer national wealth and property from foreign hands to their very own. And as long as the new revolutionary governments can do this without having to pay the piper now, the fashion will continue and spread to other countries in Latin America and around the world. As long as it seems easy and free to transfer foreign-owned property to the local government, there will be no stopping the practice for some considerable time to come. Our insistence on prompt and adequate compensation from the government involved, which it is neither able nor willing to pay, places us on record not only against confiscation of American property but against the changes the government is proposing to bring about. We end up accused of being opposed to social change. We come out of the controversy poorer and with less prestige. Somehow confiscation must cease to be fashionable and we must not seem to stand in the path of needed reform.

The way out of the difficulty is a simple one. If it were adopted as a unilateral and later, through treaty arrangements, as a multilateral policy, it would both turn the tide of fashion in the matter of confiscation and at the same time place us in a position to support efforts to modernize the semi-feudal societies in Latin America.

The idea suggested is twofold. To be effective, both parts of the program must be fully realized. The first part is the enunciation and immediate implementation of a policy of placing a temporary repayment tax on all imports from the country or countries involved in the confiscation. The funds thus derived would be used to pay for the confiscated property. In the case of Cuba, this would have included a tax on sugar, tobacco, citrus fruits, and all other products sold to the United States. The tax would be imposed only until the confiscation had been paid for. A joint commission with an impartial chairman would be charged with assessing the value of the properties seized.

This policy ought to be universally applicable, almost automatic in its operation. It would act as a kind of insurance for foreign investors. It would make possible the transfer of foreign-owned property to national hands without rancor or bitterness. The government undertaking the confiscation would have to accept the responsibility of living with a lower income from exports than its predecessors until such time as the confiscated properties had been paid for. It would facilitate confiscation but it would reduce its likelihood. Confiscation would lose its attractiveness and might well cease to appeal to revolutionary governments.

This, however, is only one part of the proposal. The other is that this new policy should be coupled with the announcement that the United States will support the governments in their efforts to improve social and economic conditions. Even while the compensation tax imposed for the payment of foreign properties is being collected, we should encourage both private and public financial institutions to extend aid to the new government in its constructive programs. This support of the reform effort would include encouragement of private investment and other forms of aid if the new government should desire foreign capital or technical assistance.

With such a program the United States would place itself in the position of living with the convulsive nationalism and the social upheavals which characterize our time, without being charged with protecting the status quo and opposing changes it cannot control. We would no longer have to insist upon immediate payment as a condition of friendly relations and we would not have to adopt punitive methods. In fact, the knowledge that the properties confiscated would be paid for would give confidence to American investors and the prospect of a lower income would reduce the urge to seize American properties. At the same time governments affected by this policy would be given a way of dealing with the issue of permanent foreign holdings in their countries which could be mutually acceptable.

If such a program were quickly adopted and consistently applied, it might change the character of contemporary revolutions. It might give us an opportunity to be helpful without being considered intrusive and perhaps make us seem more understanding and acceptable to the generation in Latin America bent on reforming the society they inherited from their forefathers.

INDEX

FRANK TANNENBAUM was born in Poland in 1893. He attended Columbia College, receiving the A.B. degree in 1921. In 1927 he received his Ph.D. from the Robert Brookings Graduate School in Economic and Political Science. He taught at Cornell and lectured at Yale. From 1936 until his retirement in 1961 he was Professor of Latin American History at Columbia University.

Over the years Professor Tannenbaum has worked and lectured in Latin America and by one means or another (on mule and afoot, for instance) has traveled the entire region. He has been a newspaper correspondent in Mexico, and a member of various Latin American and North American governmental or private commissions.

Earlier books by Frank Tannenbaum include *The Labor Movement* (1921), *The Mexican Agrarian Revolution* (1928), *Peace by Revolution* (1933), *Whither Latin America?* (1934), *Slave and Citizen* (1947), and *Mexico: The Struggle for Peace and Bread* (1950).

This book is set in Caledonia, a Linotype face designed by W. A. Dwiggins. Caledonia belongs to the family of printing types called "modern face" by printers—a term used to mark the change in style of type-letters that occurred about 1800. Caledonia borders on the general design of Scotch Modern, but is more freely drawn than that letter.